QUESTION BANK

Vol 1

JAR-FCL
Type Examples

Pooleys Flight Equipment Ltd
Elstree Aerodrome Herts UK
Telephone   0208 953 4870
Facsimile   0208 953 5219

QUESTION BANK

Vol 1

by Mike Burton

General Knowledge

Systems

Powerplants

Instruments

Electrics

Electronics

Mass & Balance

Performance

Principles of Flight

Propellers

Preface

The questions contained within this book are representative of the questions that may be encountered in the J.A.R examination. The objectives of the book are to draw your attention to the level of detailed knowledge and breadth of knowledge required to achieve a pass in the J.A.R examinations.

It is very important that the student should practice the reading of questions, and answering the question that has been asked. Do not assume the question has asked anything more than it really has. Study hard, regularly, and practice question answering regularly.

Good Luck with your studies, and your future. I wish you well!

Mike Burton
Aviation Instructor
Author and Consultant.

CONTENTS

Aircraft General Knowledge. Airframes, Systems, and Powerplants. Paper 1
Aircraft General Knowledge. Airframes, Systems, and Powerplants. Paper 2

Which Include:

> Airframes
> Hydraulics
> Undercarriages.
> Tyres.
> Brakes.
> Air-conditioning.
> Pressurisation.
> Fuel.
> Fuel Systems.
> Fuelling Precautions.
> Powerplants. (Piston and Gas Turbine Engines)

Aircraft General Knowledge - Instruments, Electrics and Electronics Paper 1
Aircraft General Knowledge - Instruments, Electrics and Electronics Paper 2

Which Include:

> Instruments
> Electronic Flight Instruments.
> Autoflight.
> Autoland.
> Electrical Supplies.
> Logic
> Semi Conductors.
> Flip Flops.
> Electronics.

Loading - Paper 1.
Loading Mass & Balance - Section II
Performance - Paper 1.
Performance Aeroplanes - Section II
Principles of Flight - Paper 1
Principles of Flight - Paper 2

Which Include:

> Theory of Flight
> Controls
> Duplicate Inspections
> Transonic Flight.
> Supersonic Flight.
> Propellers

Technical General Paper 1

Principles of Flight.
Systems.
Structures.
Undercarriages.
Tyres.
Brakes.
Hydraulics
Air Conditioning and Pressurisation.
Instruments.
Electrics

1. On an aircraft which employs stressed skin construction:-

   a)   the skin of the airplane takes no part of the load.
   b)   the skin of the airplane takes all of the structural load.
   c)   the aircraft skin is designed to take part of the load.
   d)   the skin is fabric which is stretched over a structure, which in turn takes all of the load.

2. Aircraft wing construction which employs the principle of the skin taking part of the load is termed:-

   a)   Monocoque.
   b)   Stressed Skin.
   c)   Semi Monocoque.
   d)   Warren or Box Girder.

3. The component of an aircraft wing which can be considered to be the primary structural member is called:-

   a)   the rib.
   b)   the main spar.
   c)   the control surface spar.
   d)   the lateral datum.

4. The Control Surfaces on a wing are usually attached to:-

   a)   the main spar.
   b)   the rear spar.
   c)   the torque tube.
   d)   the wing trailing edge stiffeners.

5. On what type of structure does the skin take none of the structural load?:-

   a)   stressed skin.
   b)   monocoque.
   c)   box or warren girder.
   d)   semi monocoque.

6. In normal flight, what is the position of the Emergency Lighting Switch?:-

   a)   ON
   b)   OFF.
   c)   OPEN.
   d)   ARMED.

7. In flight, what activates emergency lighting?:-

 a) Crew selected ON / OFF switch.
 b) Cabin altitude.
 c) Main electrical supply failure.
 d) Light intensity.

8. What is a disadvantage of an Aircraft Thermal De-icing System?:-

 a) Leakage's of hot air may damage other systems.
 b) They can only be selected 'ON' in flight.
 c) They are only effective in light / moderate icing conditions.
 d) They cannot be used during take off when full engine power is required.

9. When Anti Icing Fluid is applied to an aircraft, which of the following icing conditions would give the longest holdover times?:-

 a) Rain on a cold soaked wing.
 b) Snow.
 c) Freezing Fog.
 d) Frost.

10. Which of the following portable hand held fire extinguishers are most suitable for electrical fires?:-

 a) Foam.
 b) Dry Powder.
 c) BCF.
 d) Water Gas.

11. What type of gas is used to inflate life saving jackets?:-

 a) CO_2.
 b) Compressed Air.
 c) Nitrogen.
 d) Helium.

12. When an aircraft is being fuelled with AVTUR, which of the following is not permitted?:-

 a) Passengers embarking.
 b) APU running.
 c) Minor servicing.
 d) GPU being connected.

13. Fuel AVGAS 100LL is coloured:-

 a) Green.
 b) Blue.
 c) Red.
 d) Yellow.

14. Prior to fuelling an aircraft, which of the following precautions must be carried out?:-

    a)   The fuelling hose must be bonded to the aircraft immediately after fuel tank caps are removed.

    b)   The fuelling hose must be earthed to the nose undercarriage before tank caps are removed.

    c)   The fuelling hose must be bonded to the aircraft structure prior to removal of fuel tank caps.

    d)   The fuelling hose must be earthed to ground at all times.

15. When fuelling an aircraft, what action may be taken to reduce the build up of static electricity?:-

    a)   To keep the fuelling hose as short as possible.

    b)   To reduce the flow rate of the fuel.

    c)   To increase the flow rate of the fuel.

    d)   To use a long fuelling hose.

16. The aircraft fuelling point for AVGAS 100LL is coloured:-

    a)   blue.

    b)   red.

    c)   black on white.

    d)   white on red.

17. The principle of operation of Pneumatic Airborne De-icing Systems (Overshoes) is:-

    a)   the direction of hot air through rubber tubes to melt formations of ice.

    b)   the direction of compressed air through inflatable rubber tubes which break up ice formations.

    c)   the direction of hot air over the external wing leading edge to melt ice formations.

    d)   the flow of hot air through leading edge ducts to dissipate ice accumulations.

18. Excessive temperature within the ducts of an Airborne Thermal De-icing System is indicated by:-

    a)   overtemperature warning lights.

    b)   yellow flags on the control panel.

    c)   red flags on the control panel.

    d)   a flashing blue light on the central warning panel.

19. The primary detection instruments for carburettor icing on an aircraft fitted with a fixed pitch propeller are:-

    a)   the airspeed indicator and rpm gauge.

    b)   the rpm gauge and cylinder head temperature gauge.

    c)   the manifold pressure gauge and the rpm gauge.

    d)   the air speed indicator, rpm gauge and CHT gauge.

20. Carburettor icing is most likely to occur:-

a) at low power settings
b) at high power settings.
c) at low temperature with low humidity.
d) at high altitude.

21. On an aircraft equipped with a fixed pitch propeller, in flight, the onset of carburettor icing will first be indicated by:-

a) a drop in manifold pressure.
b) a rapid reduction in cylinder head temperature.
c) an increase in cylinder head temperature.
d) a slight drop in rpm.

22. On an aircraft fitted with a constant speed propeller, in flight, the first indications of carburettor icing will be:-

a) an increase in cylinder head temperature.
b) a drop in manifold pressure.
c) a slight drop in engine rpm.
d) a small increase in propeller rpm.

23. Serious carburettor icing in flight is most likely to occur, with a relative humidity of 40% at + 10°C, when:-

a) at engine cruise power.
b) at any engine power.
c) using descent power.
d) the engine is at ground idle.

24. A milky appearance at the sight glass of a hydraulic reservoir is an indication of:-

a) air in the system fluid.
b) pressure bleeding is occurring.
c) water contamination.
d) excessive fluid pressure.

25. What is the most probable cause of insufficient extension of an oleo pneumatic shock absorber?:-

a) low oil level with correct air pressure.
b) low oil level and low air pressure.
c) high oil level with air pressure correct.
d) low air pressure.

26. Fuelling of aircraft should not take place:-

a) when the APU is running.
b) within 60m of HF Radio or Radar equipment.
c) with passengers on board if there are 30 seats or less.
d) with passengers on board if there are 20 seats or less.

27. How is the main undercarriage normally locked in the DOWN position?:-

a) Hydraulic pressure and mechanical lock.
b) Hydraulic pressure.
c) Hydraulic pressure and a geometric lock.
d) A geometric lock and a mechanical lock.

28. The emergency lowering of the alighting gear on large aircraft following hydraulic system failure is achieved:-

a) with the use of emergency hydraulic accumulators.
b) with hand pump operation.
c) by gravity operation.
d) with the use of compressed air or nitrogen stored in a cylinder.

29. During aircraft fuelling operations .... and ....-

a) limited maintenance may be carried out - testing of electrical, radio and radar equipment is prohibited.
b) no maintenance is to be carried out - only the vital bus-bar must be live.
c) no maintenance is to be carried out - all electrical power must be OFF.
d) limited maintenance may be carried out - NO SMOKING and SEAT BELT lights must be ON in the cabin.

30. Tyre creep is most likely to occur:-

a) when the tyre is over-inflated.
b) when the tyre is newly fitted.
c) when the tyre tread is worn to its limits.
d) when the tyres shelf life limit is reached.

31. Smoke detectors are fitted, in which of the following area's:-

a) Passenger cabin, flight deck baggage compartments and toilets.
b) Passenger cabin, wheel wells, freight holds, toilets and APU bay.
c) Leading edge ducts, toilets, freight holds, baggage and equipment bays.
d) Freight holds, toilets, equipment bays and baggage compartments.

32. An automatic toilet fire extinguisher is activated by:-

a) odour detection.
b) CO_2.
c) heat detection.
d) smoke detection.

33. Discharge of an "Engine Bay" fire extinguisher, due to excessive internal pressure, is indicated by:-

a) a coloured disc tell-tale indicator on the aircraft or nacelle skin.
b) a protruding pin or ruptured disc at the bottle discharge head.
c) discolouration of the bottle.
d) foam deposits on the tarmac beneath the aircraft.

34. A CO_2 fire extinguisher is unsuitable for use on wheel brake fires because:-

a) CO_2 will not extinguish burning brake pad material.
b) CO_2 may cause an explosion when applied to a hot wheel brake.
c) electrics are not contained within the wheel brake assembly
d) only foam is suitable for use on wheel brakes.

35. What are the minimum instrument indications required for an aircraft oxygen system?:-

a) Pressure, Flow and Contents.
b) Dilution rate, Oxygen Flow, and Contents.
c) Flow, Pressure, Dilution Rate and Content.
d) Oxygen Flow and Contents.

36. Chemical oxygen generators:-

a) once started can be stopped by control selection on the flight deck.
b) produce oxygen flow when the masks are in the half hung position.
c) deliver a low pressure continuous flow of oxygen.
d) deliver a low pressure continuous diluted flow of air / oxygen.

37. Which of the following portable fire extinguishers are suitable for electrical fires?:-

a) Dry Powder, Foam, CO_2 and Methyl Bromide.
b) CO_2, BCF and Halon.
c) CO_2, Dry Powder, BCF, Halon and Methyl Bromide.
d) Water Gas, Dry Powder, CO_2 and BCF.

38. The most probable cause of main wheel shimmy is:-

a) shock absorber extension low.
b) worn torque links or toggles.
c) low tyre inflation pressure.
d) excessive shock absorber extension.

39. When the main undercarriage gear is selected 'DOWN' in flight, it is locked down by:-

a) Hydraulic down locks.
b) locking pins with warning flags.
c) sequence valves.
d) spring loaded lock jacks imposing a geometric lock on the side stays or drag struts.

AIRCRAFT GENERAL KNOWLEDGE

ANSWERS

1. - c	21. - d
2. - c	22. - b
3. - b	23. - c
4. - b	24. - a
5. - c	25. - d
6. - d	26. - d
7. - c	27. - d
8. - a	28. - d
9. - d	29. - a
10. - c	30. - b
11. - a	31. - d
12. - d	32. - c
13. - b	33. - a
14. - c	34. - b
15. - b	35. - d
16. - b	36. - c
17. - b	37. - b
18. - a	38. - b
19. - a	39. - d
20. - a	

40. Which of the following are considered to be suitable characteristics of a hydraulic fluid?:-

a) have a high flash point, low freezing point, be free flowing at all temperatures and be virtually incompressible.

b) have a low freezing point, high flash point, not affect or be affected by materials in the system and be compressible.

c) have good lubricating qualities, a high flash point, low freezing point and be coloured red.

d) have a high flash point, good lubricating qualities, be compressible and free from sludge.

41. The presence of a film of oil on the ram of a hydraulic jack, or actuator, when checked prior to flight:-

a) is for lubrication purposes.

b) is to prevent ice forming on the ram.

c) is to prevent corrosion taking place.

d) is an indication of a leaking seal.

42. Why, in some hydraulic systems, is a one way restrictor fitted in the up line of an alighting gear hydraulic circuit?:-

a) to prevent cavitation in the up line when the alighting gear is selected down.

b) to prevent cavitation in the down line when the alighting gear is selected up.

c) to prevent cavitation in the up and down line when the alighting gear is selected down.

d) to prevent cavitation in the down line when the alighting gear is selected down.

43. Hydraulic fluid expands with increased temperature. How is damage prevented to a hydraulic system, due to thermal expansion, during normal operation?:-

a) by fitting vent valves to the system.

b) by the operation of the automatic cut out valve.

c) by full flow pressure relief valves.

d) it is taken care of within the system.

44. In a hydraulic reservoir with a stack pipe fitted, the pipe line to the emergency pump is connected to:-

a) the bottom of the reservoir.

b) the base of the stack pipe.

c) the top of the stack pipe.

d) the return.

45. What is the purpose of a hydraulic accumulator?:-

a) to store fluid under pressure for emergency use only.

b) to give initial impetus when a selection is made and damp out pump pulsation's.

c) to prevent hydraulic hammering of an actuator or jack.

d) to provide initial impetus when a selection is made and store air under pressure for pneumatic systems.

46. In general terms, where in a hydraulic system is a pressure filter located?:-

a) between the main pump and reservoir.
b) in the return line to the reservoir.
c) in the suction line.
d) in the main supply, downstream of the main pump.

47. What is the most probable cause of hydraulic hammering in an aircraft hydraulic system in flight?:-

a) low accumulator fluid pressure.
b) low accumulator gas pressure.
c) low reservoir fluid level
d) low reservoir gas pressure.

48. In which of the following locations within an aircraft hydraulic system might a full flow pressure relief valve be fitted?:-

a) between the pump and the reservoir.
b) in the return line.
c) between the pump and main stream accumulator.
d) in the supply line between the reservoir and pump.

49. Which of the following methods are used to lower the alighting gear in the event of main hydraulic system failure in flight?:-

a) Fluid stored under pressure in a cylinder.
b) compressed air stored in a cylinder.
c) hand pump.
d) accumulator.

50. In the event a hydraulic accumulator has no gauge, which of the following would allow the correct gas pressure to be ascertained?:-

a) hand pump and main system pressure gauge.
b) hand pump, stop watch and main system pressure gauge.
c) main pumps running.
d) hand pump, stop watch, main system pressure gauge and shuttle valve closed.

51. Aircraft on board cabin chemical oxygen generators are designed to automatically drop to their half hung position when:-

a) the cabin altitude increases to 10,000 ft.
b) the cabin altitude reaches 16,000 ft.
c) the cabin fills with smoke.
d) the cabin altitude reaches 14,000 ft.

52. A chemical on board oxygen generating system provides:-

    a)   low pressure oxygen on demand.
    b)   high pressure continuous flow oxygen/air mix.
    c)   high pressure continuous 100% oxygen flow.
    d)   low pressure continuous flow oxygen.

53. The colour of an American oxygen cylinder is:-

    a)   black with a white hemispherical end.
    b)   white with a black hemispherical end.
    c)   green with a white hemispherical end.
    d)   green.

54. When a portable oxygen set is selected to 'Normal' it will provide:-

    a)   100% continuous flow oxygen for 60 minutes.
    b)   diluted oxygen on demand for 60 minutes.
    c)   100% oxygen on demand for 30 minutes.
    d)   100% oxygen on demand for 60 minutes.

55. A crew narrow panel oxygen regulator, when selected to 100% oxygen will provide:-

    a)   100% pressure oxygen to the mask.
    b)   100% oxygen on demand.
    c)   100% oxygen in an emergency.
    d)   100% diluted oxygen on demand.

56. An aircraft is maintaining level flight and its cabin altitude is increasing:-

    a)   the cabin pressure differential will increase.
    b)   the maximum cabin pressure differential will increase.
    c)   the cabin pressure differential will reduce.
    d)   the cabin pressure differential will remain constant.

57. On landing, the cabin pressure is equalised with atmospheric pressure by the operation of:-

    a)   alighting gear down selection.
    b)   squat switches which open the outflow or discharge valves at touch down.
    c)   squat switches which open the dump valves at touch down.
    d)   the alighting gear reaching the fully extended position.

58. In a Bleed Air (Bootstrap) air conditioning system, where is the water extractor located?:-

    a)   upstream of the cold air unit turbine.
    b)   downstream of the cold air unit turbine.
    c)   downstream of the cold air unit compressor.
    d)   upstream of the cold air unit compressor.

59. A ruptured red disc on the nacelle skin of a gas turbine engine bay fire extinguisher indicates:-

   a) the extinguisher is overcharged and therefore overpressurised.
   b) that excess pressure has been released from the extinguisher to return it to within safe limits.
   c) the extinguisher has discharged due to excess pressure.
   d) that the extinguisher pneumatic firing system has been activated.

60. Which of the following portable fire extinguishers are most suitable for an engine start fire.?:-

   a) Chemical Dry Powder.
   b) Foam.
   c) Methyl Bromide
   d) CO_2

61. What is the colour code of a portable hand held water fire extinguisher?:-

   a) Black.
   b) Green with red letters.
   c) Red with black letters.
   d) Red.

62. When an engine bay fixed fire extinguisher is activated, to what location is the extinguishant directed?:-

   a) the engine intake.
   b) the low pressure end of the outside of the engine compressor.
   c) into the combustion chambers.
   d) the high pressure end of the engine turbine.

63. AVGAS 100LL is coloured .... and has ....resistance to detonation than AVGAS 100L.

   a) blue   -   less.
   b) green   -   the same.
   c) blue   -   greater.
   d) blue   -   the same.

64. AVTUR Jet A1:-

   a) is coloured blue.
   b) is coloured clear to light straw (pale yellow).
   c) is always light straw in colour.
   d) is red in colour.

65. In an aircraft low pressure refuelling system, what is fitted to prevent a fuel tank from becoming overpressurised?:-

a) low level float switches.
b) high level float switches.
c) vent valves.
d) fuel hose pressure relief valves.

66. In the event an APU is required to be running during fuelling operations, which of the following precautions must be observed?:-

a) the APU must be shut down (switched off) while fuel is being transferred to the aircraft.
b) the APU must be started before fuel tank caps are removed.
c) the APU must be started after fuel tank caps are removed.
d) the APU can only be run if it is fitted with an exhaust extension, 6m in length.

67. Why are baffles fitted to aircraft fuel tanks?:-

a) to direct fuel to the main supply.
b) to assist in cooling the fuel tank.
c) to assist in heating the fuel tank.
d) to equalise fuel pressure within the tank, so preventing surge.

68. What will be the affect on the indicated fuel contents if a capacitive system fuel contents gauge fails in flight?:-

a) the gauge will fluctuate between high and low contents.
b) the gauge will indicate full scale deflection low.
c) the gauge will remain in the last fixed position.
d) the gauge will remain in the high position.

69. A fuel system booster pump, other than pumping fuel to the engine may also be used for:-

a) transfer and heating of the fuel.
b) transfer and jettison of the fuel.
c) jettisoning and heating of the fuel.
d) jettisoning the fuel and as an emergency pump in the event of main pump failure.

70. A red band painted on the wall of a tyre is a :-

a) light spot.
b) balance mark.
c) heavy spot.
d) creep mark.

71. The rated pressure of an aircraft tyre is the:-

a) loaded pressure when the tyre is cold.
b) unloaded pressure when the tyre is hot.
c) loaded pressure when the tyre is hot.
d) unloaded pressure when the tyre is cold.

72. The rated pressure of an aircraft tyre is recommended by:-

    a) the aircraft operator.
    b) the Aviation Authority of the country from which the aircraft operates.
    c) the European Aviation Authority.
    d) the tyre manufacturer.

73. A ribbed tyre is worn to its limits when it is worn to:-

    a) 4mm from the bottom of the wear indicator grooves.
    b) 2mm from the bottom of any groove.
    c) 4mm from the bottom of any groove.
    d) 2mm from the bottom of the wear indicator grooves.

74. An advantage of a nosewheel undercarriage configuration over a tailwheel configuration is:-

    a) a reduced landing speed.
    b) reduced possibility of nose-over in a crosswind.
    c) reduced aircraft weight.
    d) less complex construction of the undercarriage.

75. Aircraft nose wheel shimmy is:-

    a) rapid oscillation of the wheel about the wheel axis.
    b) commonly caused low shock absorber gas pressure.
    c) oscillation of the wheel about its track.
    d) rapid vertical displacement of the wheel due to uneven ground.

76. A fire of the aircraft's wheel, or wheelbrake will require which of the following types of portable hand held fire extinguishers to be used?:-

    a) CO_2 or BCF
    b) CO_2.
    c) Foam.
    d) Dry Powder.

77. A retractable main undercarriage unit is locked down by:-

    a) hydraulic pressure.
    b) torque links.
    c) a mechanical lock and a spring loaded over-centre lock.
    d) a hydraulic lock and mechanical lock.

78. The principle of operation of an oleo pneumatic shock absorber (shock strut) employs:-

    a) oil and spring.
    b) oil and air (or nitrogen)
    c) oil only.
    d) air and a coil spring.

79. What is the purpose of an APU (Auxiliary Power Unit)?:-

    a)   to provide additional thrust for take off.
    b)   to provide air conditioning air and electrical power when the aircraft is on the ground.
    c)   to provide air conditioning air and electrical power on the ground, and also, in an emergency, in flight.
    d)   to provide air conditioning air on the ground, and emergency electrical power in flight.

80. A wheel brake anti-skid unit is sensitive to:-

    a)   aircraft speed.
    b)   hydraulic system fluid pressure.
    c)   hydraulic system fluid pressure, and temperature.
    d)   angular deceleration.

ANSWERS

40. - a	60. - d
41. - d	61. - d
42. - d	62. - b
43. - d	63. - d
44. - a	64. - b
45. - b	65. - c
46. - d	66. - b
47. - b	67. - d
48. - a	68. - b
49. - b	69. - b
50. - c	70. - b
51. - d	71. - d
52. - d	72. - d
53. - d	73. - d
54. - a	74. - b
55. - b	75. - c
56. - c	76. - d
57. - c	77. - c
58. - b	78. - b
59. - c	79. - c
	80. - d

GAS TURBINE ENGINES

81.   In flight, combustion takes place within a gas turbine engine .... and the highest temperature within the engine is in the ....:-

   a)   intermittently   -   combustion chamber.
   b)   continuously   -   turbine
   c)   continuously   -   combustion chamber.
   d)   continuously   -   exhaust.

82.   In a gas turbine engine, high power ignition output (12 Joules) is used:-

   a)   continuously when required.
   b)   for engine starting and re-light.
   c)   for engine starting only and is time limited.
   d)   for engine starting, re-light and take-off.

83.   Of the 100% of air delivered by the compressor of a gas turbine engine, how much is used for combustion?:-

   a)   40%.
   b)   20%.
   c)   80%.
   d)   60%.

84.   What is the most probable cause of a "Hung Start" in a gas turbine engine?:-

   a)   Compressor stall or surge.
   b)   Failure to ignite.
   c)   High EGT.
   d)   The HP cock is fully closed.

85.   Where is the propelling nozzle located in a gas turbine turbojet?:-

   a)   At the outlet of the combustion chamber.
   b)   At the inlet to the turbine assembly.
   c)   At the aft end of the exhaust.
   d)   In the combustion chamber.

86.   With a given throttle setting selected on a gas turbine engine, as the aircraft increases altitude:-

   a)   engine rpm will increase and thrust will reduce.
   b)   engine rpm will remain constant and thrust will reduce.
   c)   engine rpm will increase and thrust will increase.
   d)   engine rpm will reduce and thrust will reduce.

87. Air flowing through the convergent duct in which a gas turbine axial flow compressor is located will experience:-

a) a reduction in pressure, an increase in velocity and a reduction in temperature.
b) an increase in pressure, a reduction in velocity and a reduction in temperature.
c) an increase in pressure, a near constant velocity and an increase in temperature.
d) a near constant pressure, an increase in velocity and a rise in temperature.

88. Between two respective gas turbine engine nozzle guide vanes:-

a) a convergent duct is formed.
b) the gas flow is straightened.
c) a divergent duct is formed which decelerates the gas flow.
d) a parallel duct is formed to straighten the gas flow onto the turbine blades.

89. Within a High By-pass gas turbine engine, which component produces most of the thrust.?:-

a) The hot or core engine.
b) The high pressure turbine.
c) The front fan.
d) The high pressure compressor.

90. As air flows through a centrifugal compressor of a gas turbine engine, when flowing from the eye to the tips of the impeller blades:-

a) velocity increases, pressure decreases and temperature reduces.
b) velocity decreases, pressure increases and temperature increases.
c) velocity increases, pressure remains near constant and temperature decreases.
d) velocity increases, pressure increases and temperature increases.

91. The front fan of a High By-pass gas turbine engine is driven by:-

a) the high pressure compressor.
b) the rearmost compressor.
c) the low pressure turbine.
d) the high pressure turbine.

92. When reverse thrust is selected on a High By-pass gas turbine engine:-

a) the direction of the hot gas exhaust is blocked and the flow reversed.
b) the by-pass air is blocked and redirected.
c) the by-pass air flow is reversed.
d) the hot gas and by-pass flows are blocked and redirected

93. The By-pass ratio of a High By-pass gas turbine engine is:-

a) 15 parts cold air to one part hot air.
b) 5 parts hot air to one part cold air.
c) 5 parts cold air to one part hot air.
d) equal parts hot and cold air.

94. When a gas turbine engine experiences compressor stall:-

a)   the EGT and the fuel flow increases.
b)   the EGT and vibration levels both increase.
c)   the EGT reduces and vibration increases.
d)   vibration occurs.

95. The highest pressure in a gas turbine engine is located:-

a)   in the combustion chamber.
b)   in the exhaust.
c)   between the compressor and combustion chamber.
d)   at the outlet of the combustion chamber.

96. Turbine blade creep is:-

a)   the temporary expansion of the blade when it is hot.
b)   the permanent expansion of the blade that has taken place after it has cooled.
c)   the amount by which a blade expands, due to the heat of the exhaust gases.
d)   the movement of the blade relative to the disc.

97. As the gas of a gas turbine passes through the exhaust and propelling nozzle, gas pressure .... velocity .... and the gas temperature .... :-

a)   reduces   increases   increases.
b)   reduces   increases   reduces.
c)   increases   increases   increases.
d)   increases   reduces   reduces.

98. Some multi spool gas turbine engines employ a centrifugal high pressure compressor. This has the advantage of:-

a)   enabling the engine to be made shorter.
b)   producing an engine of reduced diameter.
c)   allowing higher operating temperatures to be achieved.
d)   producing an engine that is lighter in weight with reduced overall diameter.

99. The primary factor which limits the operating temperature of a gas turbine engine is:-

a)   the pressure that can be generated within the compressor.
b)   the temperature that can be achieved within the combustion chamber.
c)   the materials from which the turbine blades are manufactured.
d)   the materials from which the exhaust is made.

100. Where in a gas turbine engine does the temperature reach its highest value?:-

a)   at the outlet of the compressor.
b)   in the combustion chamber.
c)   at the outlet of the turbine.
d)   at the propelling nozzle.

101. In a normally aspirated piston engine, as engine rpm is increased:-

    a)   valve timing remains the same.
    b)   ignition timing is retarded.
    c)   valve timing is advanced.
    d)   ignition and valve timing are advanced.

102. The ignition switch in a piston engine ignition system is located in:-

    a)   the secondary coil.
    b)   the distributor rotor arm.
    c)   the primary coil.
    d)   the contact switch.

103. If a wire becomes disconnected from the ignition switch of a magneto in flight and the other magneto is selected to 'OFF':-

    a)   the engine will continue to run normally.
    b)   the engine will stop.
    c)   the engine will continue to run at 95% power.
    d)   the engine will continue to run at reduced power.

104. The strokes of a four stroke piston engine in operating order are:-

    a)   power, compression, induction and exhaust.
    b)   exhaust, induction, compression and power
    c)   compression, induction, power and exhaust.
    d)   exhaust, compression induction and power.

105. What is the purpose of the fins on the cylinder head of a piston engine?:-

    a)   To increase the strength of the structure.
    b)   To increase the mass to absorb the heat.
    c)   To increase the surface area to help dissipate the heat.
    d)   To increase the mass to aid heat transfer.

106. On the compression stroke of a piston engine, as the piston ascends the cylinder:-

    a)   pressure increases, temperature increases, density increases and the weight of charge remains the same.
    b)   pressure increases, temperature increases, density remains the same and the weight of charge reduces.
    c)   pressure increases, temperature increases, density reduces and the weight of charge remains the same.
    d)   pressure remains constant, temperature increases and weight of charge and density remains the same.

107. A magneto impulse coupling is fitted to a piston engine to provide:-

a) a retarded spark of greater magnitude for engine starting.
b) a retarded spark for engine idle rpm and an advanced spark for higher engine speeds.
c) a flexible drive to absorb vibration.
d) automatic magneto internal timing.

108. A cylinder head thermo-couple, when connected to a temperature gauge:-

a) requires 28v DC electrical power.
b) requires no external electrical supply.
c) requires 24v DC electrical power.
d) requires 115v AC phase voltage.

109. The rotational speed of a turbine of an external supercharger (Turbocharger) is controlled by:-

a) the gear ratio between the turbine and compressor.
b) use of a variable controller.
c) the diversion of exhaust gases.
d) control of the gas flow through the compressor.

110. Piston engine pre-ignition in flight is primarily caused by:-

a) excessive engine loading.
b) very high engine speeds.
c) a very rich mixture.
d) prolonged engine running with a very weak mixture.

111. If the outlet port of an external superchargers waste gate actuator is blocked in flight:-

a) the waste gate will fully open.
b) the waste gate will be fully closed.
c) the engine will stall.
d) the engine Air/Fuel mixture will be weak.

112. In a piston engine dry sump lubricating system, the oil on leaving the engine, first passes through:-

a) the pressure pump.
b) the scavange pump.
c) the scavange filter.
d) the pressure filter.

113. In a wet sump piston engine lubrication system, the oil is normally stored in:-

a) a separate tank.
b) the engine sump.
c) the engine sump and a separate tank.
d) the engine lubrication gallery.

114. What component in a four stroke piston engine converts the reciprocating action into rotational movement?:-

    a)   the piston.
    b)   the connecting rod.
    c)   the camshaft.
    d)   the crankshaft.

115. On a turbocharged piston engine, with increasing altitude:-

    a)   turbine rpm will remain constant to maintain constant inlet manifold pressure.
    b)   turbine rpm will reduce with reducing air density.
    c)   turbine rpm will increase with increased compressor rpm.
    d)   turbine rpm will increase as the waste gate opens.

116. In an external supercharged system (Turbocharged), where is the waste gate actuator located.?:-

    a)   upstream of the waste gate controller.
    b)   downstream of the waste gate controller.
    c)   parallel to the waste gate controller.
    d)   parallel to the turbine.

117. Static boost in a supercharged engine is:-

    a)   the manifold pressure when the engine is at idle rpm.
    b)   the manifold pressure when the aircraft is stationary on the ground, with the engine at ground idle rpm.
    c)   the manifold pressure at rated boost.
    d)   ambient manifold pressure.

118. The maximum continuous boost permitted in a supercharged engine is:-

    a)   take-off boost.
    b)   rated boost.
    c)   maximum boost.
    d)   critical boost.

119. The volume of a piston engine cylinder from TDC to BDC is known as:-

    a)   the stroke.
    b)   the pressure volume.
    c)   the swept volume.
    d)   the swept distance.

120. What is a 'Squared' or 'Square Cage' piston engine?:-

    a)   an engine who's bore is equal to its stroke.
    b)   an engine who's bore is equal to the piston diameter squared.
    c)   an engine who's bore is equal to the radius of the piston.
    d)   an engine with four cylinders, forming a square which are horizontally opposed to each other.

121. The stroke of a piston engine is equal to:-

    a)   the swept volume.
    b)   twice the crank throw.
    c)   four times the crank throw.
    d)   half the crank throw.

122. As engine rpm is increased, on a normally aspirated engine:-

    a)   ignition timing will be retarded.
    b)   valve timing will be retarded.
    c)   volumetric efficiency will increase.
    d)   the weight of charge entering the cylinder will reduce.

123. In a supercharged piston engine, during normal flight, the highest pressure will exist in the inlet manifold:-

    a)   at the eye of the supercharger impeller.
    b)   in the manifold, just before the inlet valve.
    c)   in the manifold, at the outlet of the carburettor.
    d)   at the outlet of the supercharger.

124. In a turbocharged piston engine, the turbocharger impeller is driven by:-

    a)   the crankshaft via a gearbox.
    b)   the turbine via a gearbox.
    c)   the exhaust gases via a turbine.
    d)   the exhaust gases direct.

125. In a piston engine, where the induction manifold pressure is maintained at a constant value, when the aircraft is in a climb, engine power output increases. This is:-

    a)   due to a reduction in exhaust back pressure.
    b)   because the throttle valve is being opened by the automatic boost control unit.
    c)   because the induction manifold pressure, in real terms, is increasing.
    d)   due to reducing resistance on the propeller.

126. The compression ratio of a piston engine is:-

    a) $\dfrac{\text{clearance volume}}{\text{total volume}}$
    b)   clearance volume x total volume.
    c)   total volume - clearance volume.
    d) $\dfrac{\text{total volume}}{\text{clearance volume}}$

127. The Mean Effective Pressure of a piston engine is the:-

    a)   average induction manifold pressure.
    b)   average pressure exerted on the piston during the power stroke.
    c)   average pressure exerted on the piston during the compression stroke.
    d)   average pressure exerted on the piston during the four strokes.

128. A rich mixture in terms of piston engine fuel system supply to the induction manifold is a mixture of air to fuel:-

a) 20 to 1.
b) 8 to 1.
c) 15 to 1.
d) 18 to 1.

129. Which of the following affects the fuel flow to a piston engine?:-

a) rpm, aircraft speed and throttle setting.
b) throttle position, engine rpm and TAS.
c) throttle position, engine rpm and mixture setting.
d) engine rpm and throttle position.

130. What is the purpose of the diffuser in a float chamber carburettor?:-

a) To meter the fuel correctly for all engine speeds.
b) To provide a rich mixture at take-off.
c) To provide a slow running jet.
d) To either manually or automatically control air/fuel mixture.

POWERPLANTS - ANSWERS

81. - c	**106.** - a
82. - b	**107.** - a
83. - a	**108.** - b
84. - a	**109.** - c
85. - c	**110.** - d
86. - a	**111.** - b
87. - c	**112.** - c
88. - a	**113.** - b
89. - c	**114.** - d
90. - d	**115.** - c
91. - c	**116.** - a
92. - b	**117.** - d
93. - c	**118.** - b
94. - b	**119.** - c
95. - c	**120.** - a
96. - b	**121.** - b
97. - b	**122.** - c
98. - a	**123.** - d
99. - c	**124.** - c
100. - b	**125.** - a
101. - a	**126.** - d
102. - c	**127.** - b
103. - d	**128.** - b
104. - b	**129.** - c
105. - c	**130.** - a

1. An emergency portable oxygen set has:-

   a) three selections, Normal, Medium and High.
   b) three selections, Normal, High and Emergency.
   c) three selections, Normal, Medium and Emergency.
   d) two or Three selections.

2. With increasing altitude, the percentage of oxygen in the air entering the aircraft cabin:-

   a) is inversely proportional to the mass.
   b) reduces at a variable rate.
   c) remains constant.
   d) reduces above 10,000 ft.

3. A Vapour Cycle Cooling system may be fitted to enhance the cooling cycle of an aircraft air conditioning system. On leaving the evaporator, in the correct sequence, which components does the gas pass through?:-

   a) Compressor and Condenser.
   b) Condenser and Compressor.
   c) Condenser, Liquid Receiver and Expansion valve.
   d) Liquid Receiver and compressor.

4. In a vapour cycle cooling system, during normal operation the refrigerant is cooled by:-

   a) the compressor.
   b) the evaporator.
   c) the liquid receiver.
   d) ram air.

5. Which type of ACM is not suitable for operation when the aircraft is stationary on the ground.?:-

   a) Turbo Compressor.
   b) Brake Turbine.
   c) Turbo Fan.

6. What is an essential requirement in a Nose Wheel Steering System?:-

   a) Feedback.
   b) Triplicated servo operation.
   c) A follow-up mechanism.
   d) An emergency air back up.

7. If a portable oxygen set (120 Ltr) is pressurised to 1800psi and is selected to emergency, what will be the duration of supply?:-

a) Zero as there is no such selection.
b) 30 mins.
c) 15 mins.
d) 12 mins.

8. To what value are aircraft gaseous oxygen cylinders pressurised?:-

a) 1250 psi.
b) 800 psi.
c) 1800 psi.
d) 2500 psi.

9. Which of the following is correct of Chemical Oxygen Generators?:-

a) They must have a minimum duration of 20 mins.
b) They produce low flow high pressure oxygen.
c) They require a supply of 24v DC electricity.
d) Masks automatically drop to the half hung position at a cabin altitude of 14,000 ft.

10. When a portable oxygen set is selected to:-

a) emergency, it will produce a flow rate of 10 Litres per min.
b) emergency, it will produce high pressure on demand.
c) test mask, it will produce a higher pressure and flow rate than any other selection.
d) high, it will have a duration of 12 mins.

11. Which is true of chemical oxygen generators?:-

a) Once activated they cannot be stopped.
b) Low pressure oxygen is available in the 'half hung' position.
c) They provide diluted oxygen on demand.
d) They provide continuous flow high pressure oxygen.

12. During the landing run, when wheel brake anti-skid units are activated:-

a) full brake pressure is applied to the brake units.
b) brake fluid pressure is reduced by returning fluid to the reservoir via the brake control valve.
c) brake fluid pressure is reduced by returning fluid from the brake unit direct to return.
d) brake fluid pressure is reduced by returning fluid from the brake unit direct to the accumulator.

13. The purpose of a fusible alloy plug is to:-

a) slowly reduce tyre pressure if the tyre pressure becomes excessive.
b) slowly allow the tyre to deflate due to excessive temperature at the tyre.
c) slowly allow the tyre to deflate due to excessive wheel speed.
d) slowly allow the tyre to deflate if the tyre pressure is excessive due to over-inflation.

14. What considerations should be given to tyres on a large aircraft prior to landing?:-

a) Landing speed, surface contamination of the runway and brake temperature during the landing.
b) Aircraft weight, wheel rpm and brake temperature.
c) Runway surface contamination, weight and wheel speed.
d) Brake temperature and surface contamination.

15. Multi Disc brake units are assessed for wear:-

a) by measuring individual brake pad thicknesses.
b) by wear indicator pins which extend as brake wear takes place.
c) by wear indicators that change colour as brake wear takes place.
d) by wear indicator pins that retract into the torque plate as wear occurs.

16. The primary function of wheel brake adjusters is to:-

a) provide the minimum possible clearance between disc and pad when brakes are on.
b) provide the minimum possible clearance between disc and pad when brakes are off.
c) provide a running clearance with brakes on.
d) provide a running clearance with brakes off.

17. In an aircraft pressurisation system where are the blow out valves fitted?:-

a) In the air conditioning supply between the engine and pressure reducing valve.
b) In the fuselage, to relieve excess pressure in the event of mass flow control valve failure.
c) In the cabin floor.
d) In the discharge valves, and open in the event of discharge valve failure.

18. Emergency lowering of the undercarriage, in the event of hydraulic supply failure is normally achieved with the use of:-

a) compressed air stored in a cylinder.
b) spring loaded thrust arms.
c) high 'G' forces generated by aircraft manoeuvring.
d) fluid stored under pressure in an accumulator.

19. If a higher cabin altitude is required in a pressurised cabin then:-

a) the mass flow controller output is reduced.
b) the outflow valves must be moved toward the open position.
c) the discharge valves must be moved toward the closed position.
d) the mass flow controller must be moved toward the fully open position.

20. Slow, sluggish operation of a hydraulic system is:-

a) an indication of air in the system and it requires bleeding.
b) low accumulator charge pressure causing rapid system pressure fluctuations.
c) an indication of water in the hydraulic system.
d) caused by a blocked high pressure filter element.

21. Discharge of an engine bay fire extinguisher due to normal firing operation is indicated by:-

   a) a red pin extended at the base of the extinguisher distributor valve.
   b) a red ruptured disc at the base of the extinguisher distributor valve.
   c) a red ruptured disc on the engine nacelle.
   d) a yellow ruptured disc on the extinguisher.

22. When an undercarriage position light is red, what does this indicate?:-

   a) The undercarriage is locked up.
   b) The undercarriage is unlocked.
   c) The undercarriage is moving between up and down.
   d) The undercarriage is locked down.

23. To minimise tyre scuffing on large aircraft when taxying:-

   a) taxying speed should not exceed 22 kts.
   b) ribbed tyres are used.
   c) reverse thrust should be used for breaking.
   d) plain treaded tyres should be used.

24. What is the purpose of a Twin Contact Tyre?:-

   a) To reduce hydroplaning.
   b) To deflect surface water away from engine intakes.
   c) To reduce shimmy.
   d) For grass runway operation.

25. If a tyre deflates due to a fusible alloy plug blowing:-

   a) it should be removed and serviced.
   b) it should be scrapped.
   c) it should be reinflated as soon as possible to avoid damage.
   d) it may be reinflated providing it has not been run whilst deflated..

26. Side loads imposed on an undercarriage unit on landing are absorbed by:-

   a) the side load strut or link.
   b) the torque links.
   c) the shock absorber.
   d) locking pins.

27. The main undercarriage of an aircraft is normally prevented from collapsing on the ground by:-

   a) a mechanical lock and hydraulic pressure.
   b) locking pins with flags.
   c) a hydraulic lock and aerodynamic lock.
   d) a mechanical lock.

28. To what distance should a fuelling zone extend from a fuelling point or vent point.?:-

a) 15 m.
b) 50 m.
c) 16 m.
d) 6 m.

29. Avgas 100LL is:-

a) coloured green and has a higher octane rating than 100L.
b) coloured blue and has the same octane rating as 100L.
c) coloured green and has the same resistance to detonation as 100L
d) coloured green and contains less lead than 100L.

30. An aircraft Avgas fuelling point is colour coded:-

a) white with red letters.
b) red with blue lettering.
c) red with red lettering.
d) black with red letters.

31. When an aircraft is being fuelled, its APU:-

a) cannot be run.
b) may be run if the exhaust is 50 ft from the nearest fuelling point.
c) may be run if started before fuelling operations are commenced.
d) may be run if there are no passengers on board.

32. During fuelling operations:-

a) nav lights should be off and strobe lights on.
b) all external lights should be off.
c) all external lights should be on.
d) only external yellow hazard lights should be on.

33. In order to reduce static build up when fuelling an aircraft:-

a) the hose should be kept as short as possible.
b) the hose must be bonded directly to earth.
c) the fuel flow rate must be reduced from the tanker.
d) a lower octane fuel must be used.

34. Which of the following is correct when an aircraft is being fuelled?:-

a) passengers are not allowed to embark or disembark under any circumstances.
b) servicing of any kind must not be carried out
c) passengers may remain on board if the aircraft has over 20 seats and is being fuelled with AVTUR.
d) passengers may remain on board only if two air bridges are available.

35. Which of the following portable fire extinguishers are most suitable for electrical fires?:-

a) CO_2 and BCF.
b) CO_2, BCF and FOAM.
c)   FOAM, Dry Powder and CO_2.
c)   FREON, Halon and FOAM.

36. When an engine bay fixed fire extinguisher is activated:-

a)   it requires 28v DC and directs the extinguishant into the engine intake.
b)   it requires 24v DC and directs the extinguishant into the engine combustion chambers.
c)   it requires 28v DC and directs the extinguishant to the outside of the engine.
d)   it directs extinguishant to the inside and outside of the engine casing.

37. The most probable cause of rapid system pressure fluctuations is:-

a)   reservoir level low.
b)   accumulator fluid pressure low.
c)   the charge pressure of the accumulator is low.
d)   the system pressure is low.

38. One of the functions of an Automatic Cut Out Valve in a hydraulic supply system is to:-

a)   limit pump wear.
b)   prevent a hydraulic lock.
c)   prevent hydraulic hammering.
d)   maintain the fluid at a constant viscosity.

39. A Pressure Filter is fitted in a hydraulic system:-

a)   between the reservoir and pump.
b)   in the return line.
c)   at the outlet from the reservoir.
d)   after the pump.

40. A hand held portable water fire extinguisher is colour coded:-

a)   Blue.
b)   Green.
c)   Black.
d)   Red.

ANSWERS

1. - d	21. - a
2. - c	22. - b
3. - a	23. - a
4. - d	24. - c
5. - a	25. - b
6. - c	26. - a
7. - d	27. - b
8. - c	28. - d
9. - d	29. - b
10. - a	30. - c
11. - a	31. - c
12. - c	32. - b
13. - b	33. - c
14. - a	34. - c
15. - d	35. - a
16. - d	36. - c
17. - c	37. - c
18. - a	38. - a
19. - b	39. - d
20. - a	40. - d

41. Which of the following is required to check the charge pressure of an accumulator which is not fitted with a gauge?:-

a) Stop watch, hand pump and main system pressure gauge.
b) Stop watch, hand pump and adapter gauge.
c) Main system pressure gauge, flow meter and hand pump.
d) Main pump running.

42. What regulates the main hydraulic system pressure in a constant volume supply system?:-

a) The pump control piston.
b) The ACOV.
c) The pressure regulator valve.
d) The accumulator.

43. What is the purpose of a one way restrictor valve?:-

a) To prevent cavitation in the up line of the undercarriage circuit when the undercarriage is selected down.
b) To prevent cavitation in the down line of the undercarriage circuit when the undercarriage is selected down.
c) To prevent cavitation in the down line of the undercarriage circuit when the undercarriage is selected up.
d) To prevent cavitation in the up line of the undercarriage circuit when the undercarriage is selected up.

44. How is the undercarriage normally locked down on a down selection?:-

a) By a mechanical lock and locking pins with flags.
b) By a mechanical lock and hydraulic pressure.
c) By a hydraulic lock with a mechanical locking pin.
d) By a mechanical lock and overcentre lock.

45. A Hydraulic Fuse is fitted in a hydraulic system, to prevent excessive fluid loss in the event of a leak:-

a) upstream of the fuse.
b) anywhere in the system.
c) in the reservoir.
d) downstream of the fuse.

46. What indications are given that an engine bay fire extinguisher has become overpressurised?:-

a) A red pin extending at the base of the fire extinguisher.
b) A ruptured red disc or diaphragm.
c) A warning light illuminated on the CWP.
d) A yellow flag on the CWP.

47. Which of the following are the most suitable portable hand held fire extinguishers for use on engine start fires?:-

a) CO_2 - Foam.
b) BCF - Foam.
c) CO_2 - Dry powder.
d) CO_2 - BCF.

48. What fuel identification markings should be used on a tanker that contains AVTUR?:-

a) White letters on a red background with a yellow colour code.
b) White letters on a black background.
c) Black letters on a red background with a yellow colour code.
d) Black letters on any colour background with a white colour code.

49. How much fuel is required for a retained sample?:-

a) $1\frac{1}{2}$ Litres.
b) .5 Litres.
c) $2\frac{1}{2}$ Litres.
d) 2 Litres.

50. When low pressure refuelling, what prevents low pressure forming in the fuel tanks during the fuelling process?:-

a) The vent valve.
b) The minimum level float switch.
c) The maximum level float switch.
d) The relief valve.

51. When fuelling an aircraft, how can the build up of static electricity be reduced.?:-

a) By reducing the length of hose.
b) by reducing the fuel flow rate.
c) by bonding the hose to the nose undercarriage.
d) by increasing the length of hose.

52. How long will a 120 Litre Portable Oxygen Set provide oxygen when selected to NORMAL?:-

a) 30 mins.
b) 40 mins.
c) 50 mins.
d) 60 mins.

53. To what value is a 120 Litre Portable Oxygen Set pressurised?:-

a) 2800 psi.
b) 1800 psi
c) 750 psi.
d) 3000 psi.

54. Which selection must be made on a Narrow Panel Diluter Demand Oxygen Regulator to provide 100% oxygen on demand?:-

a) Emergency.
b) 100% Oxygen.
c) Test Mask.
d) Normal.

55. In Fig 1 what should be the positions of valves 1 & 2 to provide an increase in cabin temperature?:-

Fig 1.

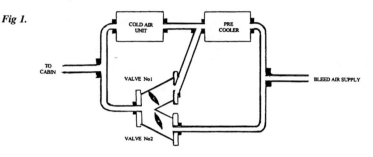

a) Valve 1. toward open   -   Valve 2 toward closed.
b) Valve 1. toward closed   -   Valve 2 toward open.
c) Valve 1. toward open   -   Valve 2 toward open
d) Valve 1. toward closed   -   Valve 2 toward closed.

56. In a Bootstrap Bleed Air air conditioning system, if the cabin temperature is reduced:-

a) The Boot Strap Compressor rpm will increase.
b) Pressure at the outlet of the cold air unit will increase.
c) Pressure at the cold air unit compressor inlet will increase.
d) The flow rate at the mass flow controller outlet will increase.

57. What is shimmy?:-

a) Movement of the wheel about a vertical datum.
b) The ability of the wheel to caster.
c) Movement of the wheel about its track.
d) Scuffing of the tyre.

58. If an aircraft is descending, what will happen to the cabin pressure differential?:-

a) It will remain constant.
b) It will increase.
c) It will remain constant until the aircraft reaches 8000 ft.
d) It will reduce.

59.   On touch down the cabin pressure will be equalised by operation of the:-

a)   outflow valves moving to the fully open position.
b)   dump valves operated by the squat switches.
c)   outward pressure relief valves.
d)   inward pressure relief valves.

60.   Light aircraft brake pad wear is measured by:-

a)   measuring individual pad thickness.
b)   measuring across the brake calliper with brakes 'ON'.
c)   measuring across the break calliper with brakes 'OFF'.
d)   measuring the wear indicator pins.

41. - d

42. - b

43. - b

44. - d

45. - d

46. - b

47. - d

48. - b

49. - c

50. - a

51. - b

52. - d

53. - b

54. - b

55. - b

56. - a

57. - c

58. - d

59. - b

60. - a

61. An aircraft piston engine is:-

    a)   a constant pressure engine.
    b)   a constant volume engine.
    c)   a variable volume engine.
    d)   a variable pressure engine.

62. A piston engine pressure injector delivers fuel to the jets:-

    a)   continuously.
    b)   on the induction stroke.
    c)   on the exhaust stroke.
    d)   on the compression stroke.

63. What transfers the reciprocating action of a piston engine to the rotational component?:-

    a)   the piston
    b)   the camshaft.
    c)   the connecting rod.
    d)   the crankshaft.

64. The condenser of a piston engine ignition system:-

    a)   prevents pre-ignition.
    b)   ensures a rapid collapse of the magnetic field.
    c)   allows arcing at the contact points.
    d)   controls ignition timing.

65. In flight, what controls the mixture of fuel to air in a fuel injector?:-

    a)   The throttle valve position.
    b)   The throttle valve position and the venturi.
    c)   The fuel pump
    d)   The venturi.

66. An advantage of a squared engine is:-

    a)   a longer stroke is achieved.
    b)   higher rpm for a given throttle setting with less vibration.
    c)   less cooling is required.
    d)   less vibration due to its increased swept volume.

67. In a normally aspirated piston engine, as rpm is increased:-

    a)   the spark and valve timing must be advanced.
    b)   the spark must be advanced and valve timing retarded.
    c)   the spark and valve timing remain in the same position.
    d)   the spark must be advanced and valve timing remain the same.

68. Which of the following will require ignition timing to be retarded in a running piston engine?:-

a) High engine rpm with low manifold pressure.
b) Low engine rpm or high manifold pressure.
c) Low engine rpm or low manifold pressure.
d) High engine rpm with a constant manifold pressure with increasing altitude.

69. The primary cause of detonation in a running piston engine is:-

a) hot spots in the cylinder head such as a hot exhaust valve.
b) running with the mixture too rich.
c) excessive engine rpm, leading to high CHT.
d) excessive pressure in the cylinder head.

70. If a wire or lead becomes disconnected from a magneto switch in flight and the other magneto is selected to off:-

a) the engine will stop.
b) the engine will continue to run normally.
c) the engine will run at reduced power.
d) the engine will continue to run at quarter power.

71. If pre-ignition is present in a piston engine in flight the corrective action is:-

a) to weaken the mixture.
b) to increase engine rpm.
c) to enrich the mixture.
d) to reduce engine rpm.

72. A mixture of 18 to 1 being supplied by a carburettor is considered to be:-

a) a rich mixture.
b) a weak mixture.
c) a very weak mixture.
d) a chemically correct mixture.

73. The ignition switch in a piston engine ignition system is positioned in:-

a) the secondary circuit.
b) the primary coil.
c) the distributor.
d) the rotor of the distributor.

74. The spark occurs in a piston engine ignition system when:-

a) the points are open.
b) the points are closed.
c) the points are starting to close.
d) the points are opening.

75. Piston engine hydraulicing may be indicated by:-

   a) blue smoke from the exhaust.
   b) black smoke from the exhaust.
   c) white smoke from the exhaust.
   d) a resistance to engine turnover when engine start is initiated.

76. For a given throttle lever setting, at rated boost, the pressure in the induction manifold of an internally supercharged engine will , up to rated altitude:-

   a) progressively reduce.
   b) progressively increase.
   c) remain approximately the same.
   d) remain exactly the same.

77. At a constant throttle setting, the power of an internally supercharged engine will:-

   a) increase with increasing altitude up to a given point.
   b) remain exactly the same up to rated altitude and then reduce.
   c) remain approximately the same up to full throttle height.
   d) reduce slightly with increasing altitude.

78. In an internal supercharged piston engine, if the outlet port of the waste gate actuator becomes blocked when flying at low altitude:-

   a) the waste gate will move to the fully open position.
   b) the waste gate will move to the fully closed position.
   c) the waste gate will not move.
   d) the safety valve will move to the fully open position.

79. Which is correct of turbochargers?:-

   a) with increasing altitude above critical height the waste gate will open.
   b) with increasing altitude up to critical height turbine rpm increases.
   c) with increasing altitude exhaust back pressure reduces.
   d) at sea level with high engine rpm at high speed the waste gate will be fully open.

80. In a wet sump piston engine lubrication system:-

   a) oil is stored in the sump and a separate tank.
   b) oil is stored in the sump and an emergency supply in a tank.
   c) oil is stored in the sump and cooled by a ram air oil cooler.
   d) oil is stored for emergency use in the sump tank.

81. In a centrifugal compressor as the air enters the eye and flows to the blade tips at the outlet of the impeller:-

   a) velocity increases and pressure energy decreases as it flows through the divergent ducts.
   b) velocity increases and pressure energy increases as it flows through the divergent ducts.
   c) kinetic energy decreases and pressure energy increases.
   d) kinetic energy increases and pressure energy reduces as it flows through convergent ducts.

82. Within the exhaust of a gas turbine engine fitted with a propelling nozzle:-

a) gas velocity, pressure and temperature remain constant.
b) gas velocity, pressure and temperature increase.
c) gas velocity, pressure and temperature reduce.
d) gas velocity increases, pressure decreases and temperature decreases.

83. The front fan of a High By-pass gas turbine engine is driven by:-

a) the LP compressor.
b) ram air.
c) the HP turbine.
d) the LP turbine.

84. In a Can Annular gas turbine combustion system how many igniters are fitted?:-

a) one on each can.
b) two on each can.
c) two to the complete system.
d) two in two cans.

85. When comparing the thrust generated by a High By-pass engine with a single spool turbojet:-

a) the turbojet produces less thrust than the High By-pass engine.
b) the turbojet produces the same thrust as the High By-pass engine.
c) the turbojet produces more thrust than the High By-pass engine

86. The High By-pass engine has a by-pass ratio of:-

a)   5:1.
b)   15:1.
c)   1:1.
d)   25:1.

87. Which is true of a High By-pass engine?:-

a) Most of the thrust is generated by the front fan.
b) Most of the thrust is generated by the "Hot" engine.
c) A major disadvantage is their greater weight compared with a turbojet.
d) They may be made smaller than a conventional turbojet.

88. A thermocouple consists of two wires of dissimilar metal and work on the principle of:-

a) a rise in the externally supplied current with an increase in temperature.
b) a reduction in the externally supplied current with an increase in temperature.
c) an emf being induced in the wires as gas flows over the probe.
d) an emf being induced in the wires by the externally supplied current.

89. The purpose of a gas turbine active clearance control system is to:-

    a)   adjust turbine blade length with variations in temperature.
    b)   eliminate turbine blade creep.
    c)   reduce turbine blade creep.
    d)   enhance turbine blade tip clearance.

90. Of the total air entering the combustion chamber of a gas turbine engine, how much is used for cooling and dilution?:-

    a)   20%.
    b)   40%.
    c)   60%.
    d)   80%.

91. Gas turbine engine thermocouples are normally fitted in:-

    a)   the nozzle guide vane inlet.
    b)   the exhaust system at the propelling nozzle.
    c)   parallel
    d)   series.

92. Gas turbine engine compressor stall or surge is most likely to occur:-

    a)   at the high pressure stages at low rpm.
    b)   at the low pressure stages at high rpm.
    c)   at the low pressure stages at low rpm.
    d)   at the intermediate stages at low rpm.

93. Gas turbine engine combustion takes place:-

    a)   at 1500°C.
    b)   at constant pressure.
    c)   at a varying pressure and temperature.
    d)   at approximately 4000°C.

94. Boyles Law states:-

    a)   The volume of a given mass of gas at constant pressure increases by 1/273 of its volume at 0°C for every 1°C rise in temperature.
    b)   The volume of a given mass of gas at constant temperature is directly proportional to pressure.
    c)   The volume of a given mass of gas at constant temperature is inversely proportional to pressure.
    d) $V \times K$ or $\dfrac{V}{K}$ = constant

95. The cold junction of a thermocouple is the:-

    a)   measuring junction and is located on the flight deck.
    b)   reference junction and is located aft of the turbine blades.
    c)   measuring junction and is sometimes known as the hot junction.
    d)   reference junction and is located on the flight deck.

96. An impulse starter is used to assist in the starting of a piston engine. What function does the impulse starter have in starting the engine?:-

a) To turn over the engine at high speed for the first two revolutions.
b) To turn over the magneto rotor at high speed to produce a greater voltage within the magneto.
c) To retard the ignition at the rotor of the distributor.
d) To increase the rpm of the distributor rotor during starting.

97. The main types of thrust reverser used on modern civil gas turbine engines are:-

a) reverse flow, clamshell door and bucket door.
b) coldstream reversal, bucket door and clamshell door.
c) bucket door, reverse fan pitch and clamshell door.
d) bucket door, coldstream reversal and recycle flow.

98. The gas flow over an impulse type turbine blade:-

a) accelerates from leading edge to trailing edge.
b) decelerates from leading edge to trailing edge.
c) accelerates at the thickest part of the blade.
d) maintains a constant velocity flow across the blade.

99. As the gas flow leaves the trailing edge portion of a turbine blade the flow is:-

a) decelerated at the throat.
b) maintained at a constant value.
c) accelerated at the throat.
d) a variable dependant on load conditions.

100. Dump valves are employed in the compressor of a gas turbine engine to:-

a) increase mass flow in the low pressure region of the compressor at any speed.
b) increase mass flow in the compressor high pressure region at any speed.
c) increase mass flow in the compressor low pressure region at low rpm.
d) increase mass flow when a surge is detected.

61. - b	**81.** - b
62. - a	**82.** - d
63. - c	**83.** - d
64. - b	**84.** - d
65. - a	**85.** - c
66. - b	**86.** - a
67. - d	**87.** - a
68. - b	**88.** - c
69. - d	**89.** - d
70. - c	**90.** - c
71. - c	**91.** - c
72. - b	**92.** - c
73. - b	**93.** - b
74. - d	**94.** - c
75. - d	**95.** - d
76. - c	**96.** - b
77. - a	**97.** - b
78. - b	**98.** - d
79. - b	**99.** - c
80. - c	**100.** - c

1. JAR 25 Electronic Flight Instrument System colour code rules require which of the following colours to display Fixed Reference Symbols?:-

    a) Magenta.
    b) Red.
    c) Blue.
    d) White.

2. The indication on an Electronic Flight Instrument System to show a system is armed is displayed in the colour of:-

    a) White.
    b) Red.
    c) Yellow.
    d) Green.

3. Cautionary information is shown on an EFIS display in the colour:-

    a) White.
    b) Yellow / Amber.
    c) Red / Magenta.
    d) Cyan / Blue.

4. Weather returns on an EFIS display show turbulence in:-

    a) Yellow.
    b) Red / Yellow.
    c) White / Magenta.
    d) Magenta.

5. In colour set 1. information on an EFIS display indicating "Fly To" or "Keep Centred" is shown in:-

    a) White.
    b) Magenta.
    c) Red.
    d) Yellow.

6. The EFIS ADI Speed Tape is located:-

    a) on the right side of the ADI.
    b) at the top of the ADI.
    c) on the left side of the HSI.
    d) on the left side of the ADI.

7. The minimum flap retraction speed is indicated on the .... side of the speed tape and shown as .... in ....:-

   a) Left - F - Magenta.
   b) Right - F - Green.
   c) Right - SRF - Green.
   d) Left - SF - Yellow.

8. The FMC / MCP Command Speed is shown on the ADI:-

   a) at the top of the speed tape in Magenta.
   b) at the bottom of the speed tape in Yellow.
   c) at the top of the speed tape in Red.
   d) to the right of the speed tape in Green.

9. When the V_1 Decision Speed is shown on the ADI and V_1 is beyond the display range it is indicated:-

   a) top right of speed tape.
   b) bottom left of speed tape.
   c) at top of command speed indicator.
   d) at bottom of command speed indicator.

10. The EFIS Radio Altitude Dial is shown on the ADI and changes from a Digital Display to a Circular Scale:-

   a) below 1000 ft AGL.
   b) at 1000 ft and below AGL.
   c) at 2500 ft AGL.
   d) at DH.

11. At what height does the DH, on the EFIS ADI display, flash yellow?:-

   a) at DH plus 100 ft.
   b) at DH momentarily.
   c) as the airplane descends below DH it flashes momentarily.
   d) from DH plus 100 ft as the airplane descends to the runway.

12. The PLAN on the EHSI PLAN MODE is orientated to:-

   a) Magnetic or True North as selected.
   b) Aircraft heading.
   c) Magnetic North.
   d) True North.

13. Which of the following statements are true:-

   a) WXR is available on all modes of the EHSI.
   b) Weather radar data is inhibited on the PLAN MODE of the EHSI.
   c) Weather radar data is inhibited on the full and expanded NAV Modes of the EHSI.
   d) Weather radar data is only available on the PLAN MODE when FULL is selected.

14. Command information is displayed in .... on the EHSI:-

a) White.
b) Green.
c) Red.
d) Magenta.

15. What are the four modes of the EFIS EHSI?:-

a) MAP, PLAN, ILS and VOR.
b) MAP, NAV, ILS / VOR and PLAN.
c) MAP, L NAV, V NAV and PLAN.
d) NAV, MAP, ILS and VOR.

16. What does this symbol represent on the EHSI MAP MODE?:-

a) Waypoint, active when magenta.
b) Airport.
c) Off-route waypoint.
d) Navaid.

17. In the event of total electrical main generator failure:-

a) both EFIS are inoperative.
b) both EFIS will continue to operate.
c) both EFIS will continue to operate with non essential EFIS signals shut down.
d) first officers EFIS becomes inoperative.

18. What is the FMCS?:-

a) Autopilot / Flight Director System.
b) Flight Management Inertial Reference System.
c) The Auto Throttle System.
d) Flight Management Computer System.

19. In the event inaccurate radio updating is exercised what effect will this have on the FMS?:-

a) This will cause the FMS to shut down.
b) This FMS will automatically update the system.
c) This may cause the FMS to deviate from the desired track.
d) This will have no effect on the FMS.

20. In an electrical circuit, what is the force behind current flow?:-

a) Emf measured in volts.
b) Emf measured in amps.
c) Amperes.
d) Farads.

21. What is the purpose of a voltmeter?:-

a) To measure current.
b) To measure pd. and is fitted in parallel with the component.
c) To measure voltage and is fitted in series with the component.
d) To measure pd. and is fitted in series with the load.

22. What are Transformers rated in?:-

a) Kw.
b) Volts.
c) KVAR
d) KVA.

23. In an electrical circuit, if the cross sectional area of a conductor is increased:-

a) resistance will remain the same.
b) resistance will reduce.
c) resistance will increase.
d) none of the above.

24. What is the purpose of an Ammeter?:-

a) To measure resistance.
b) To measure Emf and is fitted in series with the component.
c) To measure current and is fitted in parallel in the circuit.
d) To measure current and is fitted in series in the circuit.

25. In an electrical circuit with 28v, 7 amps and 4 ohms, the power is:-

a) 112 Watts.
b) 196 Volts.
c) 28 Watts.
d) 196 Watts.

26. The principle of an electrical generator is:-

a) Electro magnetic conversion.
b) Electro magnetic induction.
c) Electro motive force.
d) Electro self induction.

27. What does electric current consist of?:-

a) Heat and magnetism.
b) Magnetism and chemical.
c) Magnetism.
d) Chemical, heat and magnetism.

28. When an electrical circuit is open circuited:-

    a)   components will operate normally.
    b)   resistance will be low.
    c)   resistance will be high.
    d)   resistance will be zero.

29. In an electrical earth return circuit:-

    a)   protection devices are not required.
    b)   the battery negative is connected to the aircraft structure.
    c)   the fuse is located in the earth return.
    d)   batteries cannot be used.

30. Voltage regulation of an electrical generator in an aircraft is achieved by:-

    a)   control of the generators rotational speed.
    b)   frequency control.
    c)   real and reactive load control.
    d)   control of Field current.

31. In flight, the warning light of one of a pair of paralleled DC generators illuminates. What does this indicate?:-

    a)   Both generators are undervolting.
    b)   Excessive voltage is being produced by that generator.
    c)   That generator is disconnected from the bus-bar.
    d)   The split bus relay is open.

32. DC generators are rated in:-

    a)   Kw.
    b)   Kwa.
    c)   Kva.
    d)   Kvar.

33. In which of the following electrical circuits is a current limiter most likely to be fitted?:-

    a)   An EFIS display circuit.
    b)   A lighting circuit.
    c)   A low voltage DC circuit.
    d)   A supply circuit.

34. What are fuses rated in?:-

    a)   Volts.
    b)   Volts and Amps.
    c)   Amps.
    d)   Amps and Ohms.

35. In a 3 phase Delta connected AC generator:-

 a) line voltage is greater than phase voltage.
 b) line current is equal to phase current.
 c) line current is less than phase current.
 d) line voltage is equal to phase voltage.

36. In an inductive AC electrical supply circuit:-

 a) voltage lags current.
 b) voltage and current are in phase.
 c) voltage leads current.
 d) none of the above.

37. In a capacitive AC Supply System, if frequency reduces:-

 a) current increases.
 b) capacitive reactance reduces.
 c) current reduces.
 d) Inductive reactance increases

38. In a paralleled inductive AC Supply System, what will happen if the frequency of one generator reduces?:-

 a) Inductive reactance will increase.
 b) this will have no effect on the supply system.
 c) high circulating current will exist in the real load.
 d) circulating current in the real load will reduce.

39. When illuminated, what is indicated by the warning lights of an AC generators Constant Speed Drive?:-

 a) Excessive voltage and current.
 b) High temperature and high oil pressure.
 c) Excessive temperature and low oil pressure.
 d) Excessive temperature and low rpm.

40. What is the purpose of a battery cut-out?:-

 a) To open when the battery is fully charged.
 b) To prevent the battery discharging into the generator.
 c) To prevent the battery discharging to the bus-bar when the generator is on line.
 d) To connect the battery to the starter motor when starting the engine.

41. In an AC electrical supply system, during normal operation, the batteries are charged by:-

 a) an air driven generator.
 b) the TRU's.
 c) the generator AC Bus Bar.
 d) the essential AC Bus Bar.

42. In a Frequency Wilde AC Supply System, from what component may constant frequency AC be derived?:-

    a)   From a TRU.
    b)   From an inverter.
    c)   From a frequency wilde generator maintained at constant engine rpm.
    d)   From the APU.

43. The symbol on the right represents, on an electronic circuit diagram:-

    a)   an OR gate.
    b)   an AND gate.
    c)   an EXCLUSIVE OR gate.
    d)   a NOT gate.

44. A logic gate consists of:-

    a)   a simple two position switch.
    b)   a series of diodes.
    c)   Junction diodes and transistors.
    d)   three terminals and two current paths.

45. What does this symbol represent?:-

    a)   a diode.
    b)   a transistor.
    c)   a p&n junction.
    d)   an EXCLUSIVE gate.

46. In-puts and outputs of logic gates are generally:-

    a)   of high current.
    b)   of low current and termed signals.
    c)   of low voltage and termed pulsated signals.
    d)   of a zero current nature.

47. A transistor is:-

    a)   a p&n junction.
    b)   a p.n.p. junction.
    c)   an n&p junction.
    d)   a p.n.p. or an n.p.n. junction.

48. Semi Conductors are manufactured from:-

    a)   hiduminium.
    b)   duralumin.
    c)   germanium.
    d)   plastic.

49. A Transistor has:-

a) a single terminal.
b) two terminals.
c) no terminals.
d) three terminals.

50. In a closed loop electrical signalling system, which of the following are part of the inner loop?:-

a) Autothrottle.
b) Altitude Hold.
c) Mach Hold.
d) Stability.

AIRCRAFT GENERAL KNOWLEDGE

INSTRUMENTS / ELECTRICS / ELECTRONICS PAPER 1

ANSWERS

1. - d	26. - b
2. - a	27. - d
3. - b	28. - c
4. - c	29. - b
5. - b	30. - d
6. - d	31. - c
7. - b	32. - a
8. - a	33. - d
9. - a	34. - c
10. - b	35. - d
11. - c	36. - c
12. - d	37. - c
13. - b	38. - c
14. - d	39. - c
15. - b	40. - b
16. - d	41. - b
17. - d	42. - b
18. - d	43. - b
19. - c	44. - c
20. - a	45. - b
21. - b	46. - b
22. - d	47. - d
23. - b	48. - c
24. - d	49. - d
25. - d	50. - d

1. In a Turn and Balance Indicator, the gyro is spinning at a greater speed than normal. What will the effect be on the indicated rate of turn?:-

    a) It will overread.
    b) It will be more accurate than usual.
    c) It will cause more precession and rigidity.
    d) It will underread.

2. In a Remote Indicating Compass, direction sensing is achieved by means of:-

    a) a detector unit which is attached to the aircraft structure and senses the value of DIP to establish the aircraft position in the earth's field.
    b) a magnet mounted in the unit which is always located in the port wing.
    c) the RMI which acts as a master indicator, transmitting signals to the aircraft instruments regarding heading.
    d) detection of the earth's magnetic flux and uses the direction and intensity of the flux density, measured in a magnetic bar to indicate direction.

3. A bounded error in an INS system:-

    a) will produce a constant track error.
    b) will cause the ground speed to oscillate about a constant mean value, which in itself will be an error.
    c) will not increase with time.
    d) will result in all of the above being correct.

4. For which of the following errors must an ASI be corrected?:-

    a) Compressibility, density and pressure.
    b) Density, compressibility and temperature lapse rate of 1.98°C / 1000 ft.
    c) Compressibility and density.
    d) Temperature and Density at MSL ISA conditions.

5. The turning errors of the direct reading compass, when relating to the Northern Hemisphere will :-

    a) decrease when the aircraft turns towards East or West.
    b) decrease when the aircraft turns towards South or North.
    c) increase as the aircraft turns toward the SW.
    d) increase as the aircraft turns toward the NE.

6. The corrections applied to the airspeed indicator compensating for compressibility effects are:-

   a) always less than 15.
   b) fluctuating with the square root of the ISA deviation.
   c) always positive.
   d) always negative.

7. The term 'TOPPLE', when applied to gyros is:-

   a) real wander and apparent wander.
   b) wander in the vertical plane.
   c) wander in the horizontal plane.
   d) gyroscopic precession.

8. The forces which affect the balance ball in a turn and slip indicator are:-

   a) TAS, weight and centripetal force.
   b) centripetal force, attitude and weight.
   c) weight, lift vector and TAS.
   d) TAS, weight and centrifugal force.

9. Which of the following is most correct when describing a Turn Co-ordinator?:-

   a) It displays turn and pitch for a rate one turn only.
   b) It responds to aircraft bank angle as well as turn.
   c) It is suitable for a stand-by artificial horizon.
   d) It indicates the angle of bank and turn rate.

ELECTRONIC FLIGHT INSTRUMENTS

10. Weather returns are displayed, when selected on:-

    a) the Captains ADI only.
    b) a separate CRT.
    c) both the Captains and Co-pilots CRT's.
    d) the Captains HSI only.

11. Decision Height is displayed on the:-

    a) EADI, and below 2500 ft the display changes to a circular scale with a magenta coloured marker.
    b) EADI, and below 1000 ft is shown as a circular scale which is erased anti-clockwise as the aircraft descends.
    c) EHSI Map Mode, and below 1000 ft is shown as a circular display which is erased anti-clockwise as the aircraft descends.
    d) EADI, and below 800 ft changes to a circular scale which is white with a magenta DH marker.

12.   Decision Height is adjusted:-

   a)   automatically by the flight management computer.
   b)   and set on the ADI using the EFIS control panel.
   c)   and set on the ADI by use of the FMS control pad.
   d)   and pre-set automatically by the autoflight system.

13.   The symbols $\diamondsuit$ and Υ on an EFIS display, represent:-

   a)   an airport and navaid.
   b)   a navaid and waypoint.
   c)   an off route waypoint and navaid.
   d)   a waypoint and navaid.

14.   The symbol $\leftarrow$ 30 as shown on an EFIS display, represents:-

   a)   wind direction and speed.
   b)   true north and wind speed.
   c)   magnetic north and wind speed.
   d)   aircraft direction and speed.

15.   In a paralleled AC supply system, the load is measured in:-

   a)   KW / KV.
   b)   KW / KVA.
   c)   KW / KVAR.
   d)   KW / KW.

16.   Frequency controlled AC generators:-

   a)   are paralleled when only the DC is paralleled.
   b)   are not paralleled under any circumstances.
   c)   are always paralleled.
   d)   may, or may not be paralleled.

17.   Paralleled AC Alternators, when fitted to an aircraft supply system will have:-

   a)   one voltmeter for each generator.
   b)   one loadmeter which measures total system load only.
   c)   one meter which indicates both frequency and voltage.
   d)   one load meter for each generator.

18.   The output of an AC Generator is rated in:-

   a)   KW.
   b)   KW / KVAR.
   c)   KVA.
   d)   KW / KW.

19. A Rotary Inverter consists of:-

    a)   an AC Motor and an AC Generator.
    b)   an AC Motor and a DC Generator.
    c)   a DC Motor and a DC Generator.
    d)   a DC Motor and an AC Generator.

20. A fault in one phase of a three phase AC Star Connected Generator would:-

    a)   affect only the phase with the fault.
    b)   have no effect on the generator.
    c)   affect all three phases.
    d)   cause the generator to stop.

21. Aircraft standard fuses are fitted to:-

    a)   DC circuits only.
    b)   DC and AC circuits.
    c)   AC circuits.
    d)   protect wiring in battery circuits only.

22. How is a low reactive load on one AC Generator, of paralleled AC Generators, compensated for?:-

    a)   reducing the overall load.
    b)   increasing generator rpm.
    c)   altering the excitation current in its field circuit.
    d)   increasing the real load on the other generators.

23. In a supply system which is AC, DC requirements are provided by:-

    a)   a static inverter.
    b)   rotary inverters.
    c)   batteries.
    d)   TRU's.

24. What influences the speed of rotation of a synchronous motor?:-

    a)   Frequency.
    b)   Voltage.
    c)   Current.
    d)   Reactance.

25. Which of the following is correct of AC Induction Motors?:-

    a)   AC is induced in the rotor.
    b)   A DC supply produces DC at the rotor.
    c)   Magnetic fields are balanced.
    d)   the rotor is of a Star Wound type.

26. In a Three Phase AC motor, if one phase fails:-

a)   the motor will immediately stop.
b)   the motor will slow down and stop.
c)   the motor will continue to run at the same speed.
d)   the motor will continue to run at reduced speed.

27. High circulating currents on the real load of paralleled AC Generators is the result of:-

a)   an imbalance of voltage outputs.
b)   an imbalance of frequency between generators.
c)   an imbalance of field current on the reactive load.
d)   an out of balance reactive load control coil.

28. Reversing two phases of a three phase motor will:-

a)   cause the motor to stall and stop.
b)   cause the motor to reverse its direction of rotation.
c)   cause the motor to overheat and burn out.
d)   have no effect on the motor.

29. Synchronous motors are normally supplied with electrical supplies of:-

a)   direct current to the stator.
b)   three phase AC.
c)   single phase AC.
d)   AC to the rotor and DC to the stator.

30. What type of electrical circuit is usually protected using a current limitter?:-

a)   DC circuits only.
b)   circuits using current below 3 Amps.
c)   Supply circuits.
d)   Logic circuits.

31. In a split bus bar AC supply system employing non paralleled constant frequency AC Generators, which of the following will take place if both generators fail?:-

a)   No 1 TRU will supply all non-essential services.
b)   No 1 TRU will supply essential DC services; all other DC services will be lost.
c)   All non-essential services will be supplied direct from the battery bus-bar.
d)   All non-essential services will be lost.

32. In a split bus AC electrical supply system, the AC bus bars:-

a)   are connected automatically via the isolation relay, should one alternator fail.
b)   are never connected, as there is no paralleling circuit.
c)   may be connected by operation of the load share switch, which closes the relay.
d)   are connected via the bus tie breaker automatically if one alternator should fail.

33. During normal operation of a split bus bar AC supply system, the batteries are connected to:-

    a)   the vital bus bar and are charged by the generators.
    b)   the vital bus bar and are charged by the TRU's.
    c)   the essential DC bus and are charged by the TRU's.
    d)   the essential DC bus bar and are charged by the alternators.

AUTOFLIGHT

34. In a triplicated autoland system, if the loss of a channel occurs, what action must be taken by the pilot?:-

    a)   The landing may continue in manual.
    b)   no immediate action is required.
    c)   the landing should be aborted and a manual approach made.
    d)   the autoland should be deselected, reset and reselected and the landing continued.

35. Failure of a single autoland channel in a triplicated autoland system results in a redundancy status of:-

    a)   Fail Operational.
    b)   Fail Active.
    c)   Alert.
    d)   Fail Soft.

36. The critical height in a triplicated autoland system is:-

    a)   300 ft gear height.
    b)   45 ft gear height.
    c)   45 ft aircraft height.
    d)   300 ft aircraft height.

37. In a closed loop " fly by wire" electrical signalling system, Altitude Hold is a function of:-

    a)   the feedback loop.
    b)   the inner loop.
    c)   the outer loop.
    d)   both inner and outer loops.

38. An essential feature of a closed loop "fly by wire" control electrical signalling system is:-

    a)   feedback.
    b)   satellite navigation system interface.
    c)   no manual input.
    d)   single system signal channels.

39. Aircraft Central Air Data Computers (CADC) transmit data for:-

a) altitude and airspeed only.
b) altitude, Mach No and airspeed.
c) decision height, altitude and airspeed.
d) airspeed, attitude and Mach No.

40. The inner loop of an automatic flight system maintains aircraft stability by:-

a) manometric data signals.
b) INS data.
c) raw data fed to the data control bus bar.
d) aerodynamic feedback.

41. In Autoflight, a system which allows aircraft control without disengagement of the autopilot servomotors is:-

a) outer loop control only.
b) control wheel steering.
c) touch control steering.
d) manometric control steering.

ELECTRONICS

42. In electronic terms, what is a "flip flop"?:-

a) a shift register.
b) a bistable multivibrator.
c) a memory multivibrator.
d) a paralleled capacitor.

43. An EXCLUSIVE OR gate with only two inputs, which gives a high output when either input is 1, will:-

a) also give a high output when both inputs are logic state 1.
b) only give a high output when both inputs are at logic state 0.
c) give an output 0 when both inputs are high.
d) give an output 0 when only one input is at logic state 1.

44. What are multivibrators?:-

a) single stage switching circuits.
b) three stage switching circuits.
c) four stage switching circuits.
d) two stage switching circuits.

45. What does the following symbol in an electronic circuit represent?:-

a) an AND gate.
b) an OR gate.
c) a NOR gate.
d) a NAND gate.

46. Which of the following logic gates is an INVERTER?:-

a)

b)

c)

d)

47. What does the following symbol represent?:-

a) Keyboard Switch.
b) Linear Wafer Switch.
c) Toggle Switch.
d) Push Button Switch.

48. What does the symbol ⎯⎯o   o⎯⎯ represent in an electrical circuit?:-

a) Toggle Switch.
b) Wafer Switch.
c) Push Button Switch.
d) Keyboard Switch.

49. A Junction Diode:-

a) is a p-n-p junction.
b) is a p-n-p or an n-p-n junction.
c) has high resistance in one direction.
d) has low resistance in both directions.

50. Which of the following materials are considered to be Semi-Conductors?:-

a) Copper, Silver and Germanium.
b) Silver, Germanium and Silicon.
c) Polythene, Silicon and Steel.
d) Silicon, Cadmium and Germanium.

51. A Transistor has .... current paths which are ....:-

a) Three   -   Positive-Negative-Positive.
b) Two   -   Base emitter path and collector emitter path.
c) Three   -   Positive emitter path, base emitter path and collector emitter path.
d) Two   -   Positive emitter path and base emitter path.

52. Which of the following symbols represents a Transistor?:-

a)

b)

c)

d)

53. What is the principle of an electrical inductor?:-

a)   It is a conductor that accepts changing current.
b)   It is a coil which accepts changing current.
c)   It is an insulator.
d)   It is a coil that opposes changing current.

54. What does this symbol represent in an electronic circuit?:-

a)   an OR gate.
b)   a NOR gate.
c)   an EXCLUSIVE OR gate.
d)   an AND gate.

55. What is the output equal to   ?:-

a)   an AND gate.
b)   a NOT gate.
c)   an EXCLUSIVE OR gate.
d)   an OR gate.

56. What is this

A	B	C
1	0	0
0	1	0
1	1	1
0	0	0

?:-

a)   A Truth Table for logic gates.
b)   A Transistor current flow chart.
c)   A Transistor code chart.
d)   A Diode code chart.

AIRCRAFT GENERAL KNOWLEDGE

INSTRUMENTS / ELECTRIC'S / ELECTRONICS. PAPER 2.

ANSWERS

1. - a	29. - b
2. - d	30. - c
3. - d	31. - d
4. - b	32. - d
5. - a	33. - b
6. - d	34. - b
7. - b	35. - d
8. - a	36. - b
9. - b	37. - c
10. - c	38. - a
11. - b	39. - d
12. - b	40. - d
13. - d	41. - b
14. - a	42. - b
15. - c	43. - c
16. - d	44. - d
17. - d	45. - d
18. - c	46. - d
19. - d	47. - c
20. - c	48. - c
21. - b	49. - c
22. - c	50. - d
23. - d	51. - b
24. - a	52. - b
25. - a	53. - d
26. - d	54. - a
27. - b	55. - d
28. - b	56. - a

LOADING (MASS & BALANCE I)

1. With reference to aeroplanes, what is that plane from which the centres of gravities of all masses are referenced?:-

a) The Centre of Gravity.
b) The Datum.
c) The Normal or Vertical Axis.
d) The Centre of Pressure.

2. The Operating Mass of an aircraft is:-

a) the total mass of the aircraft at take-off.
b) the dry operating mass, plus fuel, but without traffic load.
c) the traffic loaded weight minus non revenue load.
d) the dry operating mass minus crew and crew baggage.

3. What is the Maximum Zero Fuel Mass?:-

a) The dry operating mass excluding traffic load and fuel.
b) The dry operating mass excluding fuel, plus traffic load.
c) The traffic load, excluding non revenue load but including cargo.
d) The maximum permissible mass of an aeroplane with no useable fuel.

4. The Take-off mass of an aeroplane is:-

a) the take-off mass subject to departure limitations.
b) the lowest of performance limited mass.
c) the mass of the aeroplane including everyone and everything contained within it, at the start of the take-off run.
d) the mass of the aeroplane including everyone and everything contained within it, at the departure from the loading gate.

5. What is the balance arm?:-

a) The distance from the C of G to the C of P.
b) The distance from the Datum to the C of P.
c) The distance from the Datum to the C of G.
d) The static margin.

6. Which of the following items are included in the Dry Operating Mass?:-

a) Fuel, Oils and Water.
b) Crew, Crew Baggage, Food and Beverages and Passengers Service Equipment.
c) Passengers, Crew, Crew and Passenger Baggage.
d) Passenger Service Equipment, Crew and Passenger Baggage.

7. What is the Regulated Take-off Mass?:-

a)   It is the lowest of Performance Limited and Structural Limited T.O.M.
b)   It is the maximum of Performance Limited and Structural Limited T.O.M.
c)   It is the maximum permissible mass of an aeroplane with no useable fuel.
d)   It is the Performance Limited Take-off Mass.

8. If the aircraft C of G is on the forward centre of gravity limit:-

a)   the stalling speed is increased.
b)   the stalling speed is reduced.
c)   the stalling speed is unchanged, provided the C of G is between the fore and aft C of G limits.
d)   the stalling angle will be increased.

9. An aircraft has two cargo holds. Hold 1 Balance Arm is +94 inches, and the Balance Arm for Hold 2 is +210 inches. The C of G limits for the aircraft are forward +156 inches and aft +165 inches. The aircraft is loaded to a Traffic Mass of 10,650 lbs and the C of G is positioned 172 inches aft of the datum. How much mass must be moved between holds to move the aircraft C of G to the aft limit.?:-

a)   640 lbs from Hold 1. to Hold 2.
b)   460 lbs from Hold 2. to Hold 1.
c)   640 lbs from Hold 2. to Hold 1.
d)   690 lbs from Hold 2. to Hold 1.

10. An aircraft has a single hold with a balance arm of 9.91 metres aft of the datum. The C of G is positioned 4.72 metres aft of the datum. The traffic load is 8420kgs. What will be the new C of G position if an extra 475 kgs of cargo is loaded into the hold?:-

a)   +4.15 metres.
b)   +5.62 metres.
c)   +4.99 metres.
d)   +3.94 metres.

11. Under what circumstances must the aircraft operator establish the mass of individual passengers and adding to it a predetermined constant to account for hand baggage and clothing?:-

a)   When the aircraft has 10 or less seats.
b)   When the aircraft has 20 or less seats.
c)   When the aircraft has 19 or less seats.
d)   When the aircraft has less than 10 seats.

12. A mass of 21,843.6 lbs = :-

    a)   109908.6234 kgs.
    b)   9908.090293 kgs.
    c)   8908.902391 kgs.
    d)   6980.93934 kgs.

13. Which of the following is correct to convert US Gallons to Litres?:-

    a)   US Gall x 3.785412.
    b)   US Gall x 4.546092.
    c)   US Gall x 3.985412.
    d)   US Gall x 0.980665.

14. The Taxi Mass is:-

    a)   equal to the take-off mass.
    b)   The mass of the aircraft at departure from the loading gate.
    c)   DOM plus fuel mass.
    d)   equal to operating mass.

15. Where the total number of seats available on an aircraft is 20 or more, the standard masses include hand baggage and the mass of an infant:-

    a)   2 years of age or below.
    b)   below 3 years of age.
    c)   3 years of age or below.
    d)   below 2 years of age.

16. On flights in an aircraft with 19 passenger seats or less, where no hand luggage is carried in the cabin:-

    a)   5 kg may be deducted from the male and female masses.
    b)   5 kg may be deducted from male masses and 6 kg from female masses.
    c)   6 kg may be deducted from male and female masses.
    d)   no deduction allowance is to be made.

17. An aircraft operator shall ensure that during any phase of operation the loading, mass and centre of gravity of the aeroplane complies with the limitations specified in the:-

    a)   Approved Aeroplane Flight Manual or the Operations Manual.
    b)   Approved Aeroplane Flight Manual.
    c)   Operations Manual.
    d)   Aircraft Servicing Manual.

18. The Standard Mass for a Flight Crew member is:-

    a)   75 kg including hand baggage.
    b)   85 kg excluding hand baggage.
    c)   85 kg including hand baggage.
    d)   75 kg excluding hand baggage.

19. When an aircraft is loaded with the maximum number of passengers, maximum cargo in the hold and full fuel mass:-

    a)   its C of G will always be within limits.
    b)   its C of G will always be out of limits.
    c)   its C of G will sometimes be within limits.
    d)   its C of G will sometimes be within limits, but its traffic mass will be exceeded.

20. The Zero Fuel Mass is:-

    a)   equal to the dry operating mass.
    b)   the dry operating mass plus traffic load, but excluding fuel.
    c)   the dry operating mass, excluding fuel, crew and crew baggage, water and catering services.
    d)   equal to the Traffic Load, excluding the fuel mass.

1.	- b
2.	- b
3.	- d
4.	- c
5.	- c
6.	- b
7.	- a
8.	- a
9.	- c
10.	- c
11.	- d
12.	- b
13.	- a
14.	- b
15.	- d
16.	- c
17.	- a
18.	- c
19.	- c
20.	- b

1. If the centre of gravity of an aircraft is close to the aft limit, which of the following will result?:-

    a)   An increase in range.
    b)   A reduction in fuel consumption.
    c)   An increase in drag.
    d)   An increase in rate of climb capability.

2. What is the dry operating mass of an aeroplane?:-

    a)   It is the aeroplane total mass ready for a specific operation excluding all usable fuel and traffic load.
    b)   It is the aeroplane total mass ready for a specific operation including the traffic load.
    c)   It is the aeroplane total mass ready for a specific operation including usable fuel and excluding traffic load.
    d)   It is the traffic load minus the fuel load.

3. The total mass of the passengers, cargo, and passenger baggage including 'non revenue' load is termed:-

    a)   Traffic load.
    b)   Operating mass load.
    c)   Passenger/Cargo load.
    d)   Zero fuel mass.

4. Under normal circumstances, the maximum total aeroplane mass on landing is the:-

    a)   Regulated landing mass.
    b)   Maximum structural landing mass.
    c)   Performance limited landing mass.
    d)   Normal landing mass.

5. If the C of G of an aeroplane is close to the forward limit, what will the effect be on the aircraft's performance in level flight?:-

    a)   A reduction in fuel consumption.
    b)   A reduction in rate of climb.
    c)   A reduced stalling angle.
    d)   A reduced stalling speed.

6. Calculate the following to establish if the following aircraft is safely loaded for take off by locating the position of the C of G.

Aircraft   -   Maximum Take off Mass = 4000 lb.
                           Maximum landing Mass = 3500 lb.

C of G Limits +18"   to   +22"
Check that the aircraft is correctly loaded for take-off.

Item	Weight(lb.)	Arm(in)	Moment	
			+ve	-ve
Basic Empty Mass	2000	+20.5	41000	
2 pilots at 170lb each	340	+4	1360	
15 gall Oil (SG 0.9)	135	-4		540
98 gall Petrol(SG 0.72)		-2		
Freight	355	+30		
Baggage	320	+60		
Total Weight				
		Total Moments		

C of G = Total Moment = 70 980 = + 18.32"
              Total   3 875

Take off mass below the MTOM
C of G between limits of +18" to +22"

The position of the C of G is:-

a)   +18.22 ins.
b)   +18.98 ins.
c)   +17.48 ins.
d)   +19.20 ins.

7. If a aircraft's C of G is on its forward limit in level flight, what effect will this have?:-

    a) Range will be increased.
    b) Longitudinal control authority will be reduced.
    c) The stalling angle will reduce with increasing altitude.
    d) Induced drag will be reduced.

8. If a twin nose wheel aircraft has a single nose wheel loading of 628 kg, and a four mainwheel undercarriage with a single main wheel loading of 5000 kg and the distance between the nose and main wheels is 8m, how far is the centre of gravity in front of the main wheels?:-

    a) 7.4m.
    b) 6.0m.
    c) .64m.
    d) .47m.

9. If the C of G of an aircraft is on the forward limit:-

    a) its range will be increased.
    b) its stalling angle will be reduced.
    c) its stalling speed will be reduced.
    d) its range will be reduced.

10. What will be the affect if the weight of an aircraft is increased?:-

    a) Its stalling angle will be reduced.
    b) Its stalling speed will remain the same.
    c) Its range will be reduced.
    d) Its range will be unaffected.

ANSWERS

1. - c

2. - a

3. - a

4. - b

5. - b

6. - a

7. - b

8. - d

9. - d

10. - c

1. In a CLASS B Performance Aircraft the TAKE-OFF distance on a dry grass (firm soil) runway:-

    a) should be factorised by x1.2
    b) should be factorised by x1.3
    c) should be factorised by x1.0
    d) should not be facturised.

2. When taking off from a runway with a 2% upslope in a CLASS B Performance Aircraft, the take-off distance should be increased by:-

    a) 5%.
    b) 10%.
    c) 15%.
    d) 7.5%.

3. TORA is the:-

    a) actual runway available for take-off.
    b) actual runway available for take-off including stopway and clearway.
    c) actual runway available required for take-off including the stopway.
    d) actual runway available minus the stopway.

4. General considerations that should be given to a CLASS B Performance Aircraft when landing include:-

    a) maximum landing mass 3650 lb minus 15% of the aircraft mass.
    b) maximum landing mass 3650 lb minus 20% of the aircraft mass.
    c) maximum runway cross wind 17 kts.
    d) maximum runway cross wind 15 kts.

5. When landing on a dry grass runway in a CLASS B Performance Aircraft with a downslope of 2%, what factorisation may be used?:-

    a) 1.2
    b) 1.3
    c) none
    d) 1.4

6. Assuming identical slope and wind component values, which of the following combinations will give the most limiting mass?:-

    a) a down sloping runway with a headwind component.
    b) an up sloping runway with a headwind component.
    c) a down sloping runway with a tailwind component.
    d) an up sloping runway with a tailwind component.

7. If the outside air temperature is +3°C, what is the maximum mass an aircraft can cruise in instrument meteorological conditions at FL110?:-

   a) 2247 kg.
   b) 2172 kg.
   c) 2366 kg.
   d) 2033 kg.

8. The field length requirements for a CLASS B aircraft where no stopway or clearway is available, the take-off distance must not exceed:-

   a) 1.25 x TORA.
   b) 1.15 x TODA.
   c) 1.25 x TODA.
   d) 1.15 x TORA.

9. Light twin aircraft, for the purpose of aircraft performance, are certified under JAR 25 as:-

   a) CLASS A.
   b) CLASS C.
   c) CLASS B.
   d) CLASS D.

10. Medium Range Jet Transport aircraft are certified under JAR 25 as:-

   a) CLASS A.
   b) CLASS D.
   c) CLASS B.
   d) CLASS E.

1. - a

2. - b

3. - a

4. - c

5. - c

6. - d

7. - d

8. - a

9. - c

10. - a

1. What will be the effect of changes of ambient temperature on the performance of an aeroplane if all other performance parameters remain constant?:-

    a) A reduction in ambient temperature will cause an increase in the take-off run.
    b) An increase in ambient temperature will cause a reduction in the required landing distance.
    c) An increase in ambient temperature will cause a reduction in the required take-off distance.
    d) A decrease in ambient temperature will cause an increase in the climb gradient.

2. With an increase of flap angle from 5° to 12°, both angles are within limits, what will be the effect on:-

    I - The required take-off run to lift off.
    II - The mean drag during the take-off run

    a) I - increased.
       II - reduced.
    b) I - remains the same.
       II - reduced.
    c) I - reduced.
       II - increased.
    d) I - increased
       II - increased.

3. When an aircraft is in flight, to achieve a greater climb angle:-

    a) the amount by which lift exceeds weight must be increased.
    b) The amount by which thrust exceeds drag must be increased.
    c) The amount by which thrust exceeds lift must be reduced.
    d) The ratio between lift and drag will remain the same.

4. If the angle of attack is increased from 4° to 8°:-

    a) the lift/drag ratio will reduce.
    b) the lift/drag ratio will remain the same.
    c) the lift/drag ratio will increase.
    d) the stalling angle will be reduced.

5. When taking off from an airfield where the field length is critical and limits the take-off weight:-

    a) a small angle of flap should be selected.
    b) zero flap should be used.
    c) a large flap angle should be selected.
    d) none of the above apply.

6. If a smaller angle of flap is selected for take off compared to a larger angle of flap selection:-

a) the stalling speed is reduced, V_2 is reduced and V_R and V_{LOF} are increased.
b) the stalling speed is increased, V_2 is increased and V_R and V_{LOF} are increased.
c) V_R and V_{LOF} are reduced and the stalling speed remains the same.
d) the stalling speed is reduced and V_2, V_R and V_{LOF} remains the same.

7. In a banked turn:-

a) the stalling angle reduces.
b) the stalling speed reduces.
c) the stalling angle increases.
d) the stalling speed increases.

8. The speed at which the aircraft wheels leave the ground during take off is:-

a) V_2
b) V_R
c) V_{LOF}
d) V_4

ANSWERS

1. - d

2. - c

3. - b

4. - a

5. - c

6. - b

7. - d

8. - c

1. The airflow over the upper surface of the wing of an aircraft in level flight compared to the free stream air will:-

   a) have the same velocity, resulting in reduced pressure.
   b) have greater velocity, resulting in increased pressure.
   c) experience a reduction in velocity producing increased pressure.
   d) experience an increase in velocity and a reduction in pressure.

2. Which of the following include the quantities which affect drag on an aircraft wing in flight?:-

   a) density, angle of attack, static pressure and velocity.
   b) density, frontal area, planform and velocity.
   c) angle of attack, frontal area shape, dynamic pressure and wing area.
   d) angle of attack, air density, indicated airspeed and aspect ratio.

3. The 'Continuity of Mass Flow' theorem at speeds, considered to be incompressible, includes which of the following quantities?:-

   a) velocity, density and area.
   b) density and the square of the flow velocity.
   c) density and flow velocity.
   d) velocity of flow and section area.

4. If the aspect ratio of a wing for a given area is decreased:-

   a) lift coefficient remains unaffected at a given angle of attack.
   b) induced drag, for a given angle of attack, increases.
   c) induced drag decreases for a given angle of attack.
   d) lift coefficient increases for a given angle of attack.

5. An increase of speed whilst maintaining level flight will result in:-

   a) the wing stagnation point moving aft.
   b) the wing lift component reducing.
   c) the aircraft C of G moving aft.
   d) the wing transition point moving forward.

6. If an elevator trim tab is in its neutral position and the elevator is moved up:-

   a) the tab will move up relative to the elevator, to maintain feel.
   b) the tab will remain parallel to the chord line of the tailplane.
   c) the tab will move down relative to the elevator applying the trim input that has been made.
   d) the tab will remain in line with the elevator.

7. A balance tab is a form of aerodynamic balance and is designed to:-

a) move in the same direction as the control surface.
b) move in the opposite direction to the elevator when it is deflected up, but remain approximately parallel to the tailplane chord line.
c) be operated direct by the control column, which aerodynamically then moves the control surface.
d) operate in conjunction with hydraulic servo units.

8. Control surface aerodynamic balance:-

a) is essential on all aircraft.
b) will decrease surface hinge moments.
c) will alleviate control surface flutter tendencies.
d) will increase surface feel therefore increasing control effectiveness.

9. What is the principle function of a leading edge automatic slat, located in front of an aileron?:-

a) To reduce induced drag at the wing tip.
b) To minimise the possibility of stall when the aileron is deflected up.
c) To increase the wing stalling angle.
d) To prevent spanwise movement of the airflow when approaching M_{crit}

10. The Fineness Ratio of a wing is the:-

a) thickness/chord ratio.
b) thickness/span ratio.
c) mean chord/thickness ratio
d) mean camber chord ratio/thickness ratio.

11. At sea level under standard atmospheric conditions:-

a) IAS is greater than TAS.
b) IAS is less than EAS.
c) IAS is equal to TAS.
d) TAS is greater than IAS.

12. The thickness/chord ratio of a wing is expressed as:-

a) a ratio.
b) a decimal.
c) a fraction.
d) a percentage.

13. The mean chord is calculated by:-

a) dividing the chord by the maximum thickness.
b) dividing the gross wing area by the wing span.
c) dividing the net wing area by the wing span.
d) dividing the gross wing area by the root chord.

14. The 'Wash Out' of a wing is:-

a) an increase in its angle of attack from root to tip.
b) a reduction in its angle of incidence from root to tip.
c) a reduction in angle of attack from root to tip.
d) an increase in angle of incidence from root to tip.

15. In a climbing turn:-

a) the angle of attack on the inner wing will be greater than the outer wing.
b) the outer wing aileron will be deflected through a greater angle than the aileron on the inner wing.
c) the angle of attack on each wing will be the same.
d) the angle of attack on the outer wing will be greater than the inner wing.

16. An Anti-balance tab moves in the:-

a) same sense as its associated control surface, to increase aerodynamic loading.
b) same sense as its associated control surface to reduce aerodynamic loading.
c) opposite sense as its associated control surface to increase aerodynamic loading.
d) opposite sense as its associated control surface to reduce aerodynamic loading.

17. A tab which remains in line with the control surface when that surface is deflected, whilst the aircraft is on the ground is a:-

a) servo tab.
b) anti-balance tab.
c) spring tab.
d) balance tab.

18. In order to reduce the control column forces required to deflect large control surfaces in flight, they may be fitted with:-

a) static balance.
b) aerodynamic balance.
c) mass balance.
d) a hinge line moved further forward towards the surface leading edge.

19. The stalling speed of an aircraft in a turn (Vm) is equal to:-

a) the basic stalling speed x the cosine of the angle of bank.
b) the inverse of the load factor.
c) the induced drag that is generated.
d) the basic stalling speed x the square root of the load factor.

20. Asymmetric Spoilers:-

a) are fitted to replace ailerons on modern transport aircraft.
b) move up or down in flight.
c) move up to dump lift in flight.
d) are a form of speed brake only used on the ground.

21. If the weight of an aircraft is increased:-

a) its Vmd will remain the same.
b) its Vmd will be increased.
c) its Vmd will be reduced.
d) profile drag will be greater than induced drag at Vmd.

22. When the angle of attack on an aircraft wing is progressively increased, the wing C of P will reach its most forward position:-

a) at the wings optimum angle of attack.
b) at a high angle of attack before the stall.
c) at the stall.
d) just above the stall.

23. The employment of vortex generators on a straight wing of constant thickness section is to:-

a) reduce spanwise airflow from root to tip on the upper surface.
b) reduce spanwise airflow from root to tip on the upper and lower surfaces.
c) reduce spanwise airflow from root to tip on the lower surface.
d) delay boundary layer separation.

24. With increasing altitude, at a constant indicated airspeed, what effect will this have on C_L and stalling angle?:-

a) the C_L will remain constant and the stalling angle will reduce.
b) the C_L and stalling angle will reduce.
c) the C_L will remain constant and the stalling angle will remain the same.
d) the C_L will reduce and the stalling angle will remain the same.

25. When an aircraft is in a state of autorotation:-

a) the outer wing is fully stalled and the inner wing partially stalled.
b) the inner wing is fully stalled and the outer wing partially stalled.
c) the inner and outer wings are partially stalled.
d) the inner and outer wings are fully stalled.

26. A swept wing for a given IAS, compared to a straight wing of the same wing area, produces:-

a) less lift, improved lateral stability and less total drag.
b) less lift, reduced lateral stability and less total drag.
c) the same lift, increased lateral stability, with the same total drag.
d) increased lift, increased lateral stability, with less total drag.

27. If the C of G of an aircraft is on its forward limit line whilst maintaining level flight, what effect will this have on stability?:-

a) Longitudinal stability will be reduced with an increased download existing on the tailplane.

b) an increased download will exist on the tailplane with an associated increase in longitudinal stability.

c) a reduced download will exist on the tailplane with an associated reduction in longitudinal stability

d) a reduction in longitudinal stability will exist with no change in loading on the tailplane.

28. A secondary or further effect of an aircraft rolling to port without design corrections will be:-

a) a yaw to port.
b) a turn to port.
c) a yaw to starboard.
d) a banked turn to the right.

29. Adverse aileron yaw may be reduced by the employment of Differential Ailerons. What is the principle of Differential Aileron operation?:-

a) the up going aileron on the down going wing moves through a greater angle of deflection than the down going aileron.

b) the down going aileron on a down going wing moves through a greater angle of deflection than the up going aileron on the up going wing.

c) the down going aileron on the up going wing moves through a greater angle of deflection than the up going aileron.

d) both the up and down going ailerons move through the same angle of deflection, however, the up going aileron produces greater profile drag than the down going aileron.

30. When accelerating through the region of transonic flight:-

a) the C of P will move to the rear and cause a nose up trim change.
b) the C of P will move to the rear and cause increased stability in pitch.
c) the C of P will move forward and cause a nose up trim change.
d) the C of P will move forward and contribute to a better L/D ratio.

31. The local Speed of Sound = :-

a) 39 x absolute temperature.
b) 39 x $\sqrt{\text{absolute temperature.}}$
c) the ratio of True Airspeed to the Mach No.
d) the absolute temperature x the TAS.

32. Which of the following devices may be incorporated in wing design, to reduce spanwise airflow on a swept wing?:-

a) slotted slats.
b) slotted trailing edge flaps.
c) vortex generators.
d) boundary layer suction.

33. What is the purpose of Auto Mach Trim?:-

    a)   to compensate for longitudinal instability at high Mach numbers.
    b)   to compensate for variations in lateral stability at high Mach numbers.
    c)   to prevent wing tip stall on swept wings.
    d)   to compensate for C of G shift in the transonic speed range.

34. When an aircraft is in a climb, the angle of climb is dependent upon:-

    a)   the excess power available.
    b)   the amount by which thrust exceeds drag.
    c)   the amount by which lift exceeds weight.
    d)   the amount by which the power available exceeds the power required.

35. When a piston engined aircraft is in a climb, at a constant IAS, with increasing altitude:-

    a)   the power required decreases and the power available remains constant.
    b)   the power required increases and the power available decreases.
    c)   the power required remains constant and the power available reduces.
    d)   the power available decreases and the power required decreases.

36. What is the effect of lowering Leading Edge and Trailing Edge Flaps in flight?:-

    a) C_L increases, C_D increases and the stalling angle increases.
    b) C_L reduces, C_D increases and the stalling angle reduces.
    c) C_L increases, C_D remains the same and the stalling angle increases.
    d) C_L remains constant, C_D increases and the stalling angle remains the same.

37. When a trailing edge flap is lowered in flight:-

    a)   profile and induced drag increases and the L/D ratio increases.
    b)   the L/D ratio reduces as induced and profile drag increase.
    c)   induced drag reduces and profile drag increases.
    d)   induced drag remains the same, while profile drag increases.

38. The CTM of a propeller is:-

a) a force which turns the blades towards coarse pitch.
b) the distance a blade moves forward in one revolution.
c) a force which turns the blades towards fine pitch.
d) a force which directly opposes the torque force.

39. Propeller blades are said to be feathered when:-

a) the blades are at fully fine pitch.
b) the blades are at coarse pitch.
c) the propeller is windmilling.
d) the blades leading edges face forward in the direction of flight.

40. A double acting propeller is one which the blades are:-

a) moved to coarse by oil pressure and to fine by spring pressure.
b) moved to coarse and fine by oil pressure with spring operation provided for emergency use.
c) moved to coarse and fine by oil pressure.
d) moved to coarse and fine by spring pressure.

41. The booster pump fitted to the CSU of a constant speed propeller:-

a) provides emergency oil pressure for feathering.
b) is electrically operated, which is used to feather double acting propellers.
c) is driven by the propeller to provide oil pressure to unfeather single acting propellers.
d) increases the engine lubricating oil pressure for propeller operation.

42. A propeller blade is twisted to:-

a) ensure equal thrust is generated along the length of the blade.
b) maintain a constant angle of attack along the length of the blade.
c) balance stress forces generated on the blade.
d) increase the effective solidity of the blade.

43. A propeller which rotates clockwise when veiwed from the front and is mounted on the starboard engine is termed:-

a) a right handed propeller.
b) a clockwise propeller.
c) an anti clockwise propeller.
d) a left handed propeller.

44. When a propeller is windmilling:-

a) thrust is greater than propeller drag.
b) the propeller rotates on a free wheel unit with the propeller drive shaft stationary.
c) the propeller will move toward the feathered position.
d) the direction of rotation will be the same as in normal flight.

45. During normal operation of a constant speed propeller, what might be the reason for no oil flow within the C.S.U.?:-

   a)   the propeller is moving to the feathered position.
   b)   the propeller is underspeeding.
   c)   the propeller is on speed.
   d)   the propeller is overspeeding.

46. When a double acting propeller is selected to 'Feather' the propeller blades move:-

   a)   from coarse through fine, reverse pitch to feather.
   b)   from course through fine pitch to feather.
   c)   from fine, ground fine pitch to feather.
   d)   from fine through course pitch to feather.

47. When an aircraft, fitted with a constant speed propeller, is in level flight and a climb is initiated:-

   a)   the rpm will increase as the blades will move to fine pitch.
   b)   the blades will move to coarse pitch and rpm will reduce.
   c)   the rpm will remain constant as the blades move to fine pitch.
   d)   the rpm will increase as the blades move to coarse pitch.

48. When maximum rpm is selected, on a constant speed propeller at take off:-

   a)   the propeller blades move to coarse pitch to generate maximum thrust.
   b)   the propeller blades move to fine pitch to allow the engine to develop max power.
   c)   the blades move to a coarse pitch to enable the propeller to absorb the high engine power developed.
   d)   the blades move to fine pitch to prevent the propeller overspeeding.

49. In flight how is the propeller of a single acting type brought out of feathered position?:-

   a)   By use of oil pressure stored in a hydraulic accumulator.
   b)   By the action of the spring in the propeller actuator.
   c)   with oil pressure generated by an electrically driven pump, with its own oil supply.
   d)   with oil pressure from the CSU booster pump.

50. Thrust forces acting on a propeller blade in flight will tend to:-

   a)   bend the blades back opposite to the direction of flight.
   b)   bend the blades in the direction of rotation.
   c)   bend the blades forward in the direction of flight.
   d)   bend the blades opposite to the direction of rotation.

ANSWERS

1. - d	26. - a
2. - c	27. - b
3. - a	28. - c
4. - b	29. - a
5. - b	30. - b
6. - d	31. - b
7. - b	32. - c
8. - b	33. - a
9. - c	34. - b
10. - a	35. - b
11. - c	36. - a
12. - d	37. - b
13. - b	38. - c
14. - b	39. - d
15. - d	40. - c
16. - a	41. - d
17. - c	42. - b
18. - b	43. - d
19. - d	44. - d
20. - c	45. - c
21. - b	46. - d
22. - b	47. - c
23. - d	48. - b
24. - c	49. - a
25. - b	50. - c

1. When an aircraft is in level flight, what are the relationships between Lift, Weight, Thrust and Drag?:-

    a)   Lift is greater than weight and thrust exceeds drag.
    b)   Lift is greater than weight and thrust is equal to drag.
    c)   Lift is equal to weight and thrust exceeds drag.
    d)   Lift is equal to weight and thrust is equal to drag.

2. In level flight the Centre of Pressure, the point through which Lift is said to act, will be:-

    a)   forward of the C of G.
    b)   at the thickest part of the aerofoil.
    c)   at its most furthest forward point it will reach on the aerofoil.
    d)   immediately forward of the separation point on the aerofoil.

3. When an aircraft is in a steady climb, what is the relationship between Lift, Weight, Thrust and Drag?:-

    a)   The lift force is greater than weight
    b)   The lift force is exactly equal to the weight.
    c)   Weight is greater than the lift force.
    d)   Weight plus the drag force is equal to the lift force.

4. When an aircraft is in a climb at a constant speed:-

    a)   the thrust is equal to the component of weight acting along the flight path.
    b)   the thrust component is less than the aerodynamic drag.
    c)   the aerodynamic drag component is less than thrust.
    d)   the thrust is exactly equal to the aerodynamic drag component.

5. What is considered to be the Optimum Angle of Attack (best angle of attack) of an aerofoil in level flight?:-

    a)   An angle of attack of 3° to 4° which produces the best lift/drag ratio.
    b)   The angle of attack at which the aerofoil produces maximum lift
    c)   The angle of attack just before the stalling angle.
    d)   The angle of attack at which minimum drag will be produced.

6. What are the two forces into which the Lift Force may be resolved when an aircraft is executing a Turn?:-

    a)   A force equal and opposite to thrust and centrifugal force.
    b)   A force equal and opposite to drag and centripetal force.
    c)   Centripetal force and a force equal and opposite to weight.
    d)   A force opposite to weight and a force equal and opposite to thrust.

7. If in level flight an aircraft has a Stalling Speed of 90kt IAS, what will be its stalling speed in a 60∫ balanced turn?:-

a) 99kts.
b) 127kts.
c) 112kts.
d) 90kts.

8. Which of the following will generate a force which causes an aircraft to Turn?:-

a) A Weight component.
b) The Rudder.
c) Engine Thrust.
d) Wing Lift.

9. What is the purpose of the Ailerons?:-

a) To provide directional control about the Normal or Vertical Axis.
b) To give Lateral control about the Lateral Axis.
c) To provide Longitudinal control about the Lateral Axis.
d) To give Lateral control about the Longitudinal Axis.

10. The primary purpose of a Trailing Edge Flap is to:-

a) cause the wing to generate more lift at a given angle of attack and airspeed.
b) increase the stalling angle of the wing.
c) increase lateral stability.
d) increase lateral stability with an increased wing stalling angle.

11. In level flight, where is the Transition Point located on an aircraft wing?:-

a) The point at which airflow separates from the wing.
b) At the point where boundary layer flow changes from laminar to turbulent.
c) At the leading edge of the wing, where the streamlines divide and flow over the upper and lower surfaces.
d) At the point where the airflow changes from subsonic to supersonic flow.

12. Normally when an aircraft is in straight and level flight, the wing Centre of Pressure acts:-

a) through the same point as the wing C of G.
b) forward of the wing C of G.
c) through the separation point.
d) aft of the wing C of G.

13. As the Angle of Attack of a wing is increased, the C of P will reach its most furthest forward point on the wing:-

a) at the stall.
b) at the optimum angle of attack.
c) just above the stall.
d) just below the stall.

14. When an aircraft is in a Steady Climb, how will the wing Stalling Angle be affected.?:-

   a)   the stalling angle will remain the same, regardless of altitude.
   b)   the stalling angle will reduce with increasing altitude.
   c)   the stalling angle will increase with increasing altitude.
   d)   the stalling angle is only affected by speed.

15. What is the effect on the Lateral Stability of an aircraft, when a High Wing is employed?:-

   a)   Lateral stability will be the same as that for a low winged aircraft.
   b)   Lateral stability will be improved because of the pendulous effect.
   c)   Lateral stability will be reduced because of the pendulous effect.
   d)   Lateral stability will be reduced because of the low C of G position of the aircraft.

16. In flight, the change of the aircrafts attitude when lowering trailing edge flaps is primarily due to:-

   a)   the change in position of the aircrafts C of G.
   b)   the change in spanwise airflow from root to tip over the wing upper surface.
   c)   the change in position of the aircrafts C of P.
   d)   the stalling angle is increased.

17. Why are Vortex Generators sometimes fitted to an aircraft fitted with straight wings?:-

   a)   to reduce spanwise movement of the airflow towards the tips on the upper wing surface.
   b)   to reduce spanwise movement of the airflow towards the root on the lower wing surface.
   c)   to delay boundary layer separation.
   d)   to reduce induced drag.

18. When an aircraft is in flight, what will be the effect of moving the C of G aft?:-

   a)   A reduction in longitudinal stability will be caused.
   b)   The result will be an increase in lateral stability.
   c)   There will be no effect on stability.
   d)   There will be an increase in longitudinal stability.

19. In a glide:-

   a)   Thrust equals Drag.
   b)   Thrust is replaced by a component of weight.
   c)   Thrust is replaced by a component of lift and weight.
   d)   Lift is greater than weight and drag.

20. When Trailing Edge Flaps are lowered in flight:-

a) the wing C of P moves forward and the stalling angle increases.
b) the wing C of P moves forward and lateral stability reduces.
c) the wing C of P moves aft and the stalling angle reduces.
d) the wing C of P moves aft and lateral stability increases.

21. Induced drag is:-

a) proportional to the square of the speed.
b) proportional to lift.
c) inversely proportional to the square of the lift.
d) increases as the square of the speed.

22. Induced drag on a wing in level flight:-

a) is uniform across its span.
b) is greatest at the wing root.
c) is greatest at the tip.
d) is greatest at the leading edge.

23. Induced drag:-

a) increases with increased aspect ratio.
b) increases as the square of the speed.
c) reduces with increased tip chord.
d) increases with reduced aspect ratio.

24. A high aspect ratio wing:-

a) has a long span and short chord.
b) has a short span and short chord.
c) has a long span and long chord.
d) has a short span and long chord.

25. A wing leading edge extension is fitted to:-

a) reduce the tendency of the wing to stall at its tip.
b) reduce boundary layer flow toward the root.
c) eliminate wing tip vortices.
d) ensure the wing stalls at its tip first.

26. Aileron flutter is most likely to occur on a wing of:-

a) flexible structure with rigid ailerons at low speed.
b) flexible structure with rigid ailerons at high speed.
c) rigid structure with flexible ailerons at low speed.
d) rigid structure with flexible ailerons at high speed.

27. Reduction of flutter may be achieved with the use of:-

a) horn balance.
b) frise ailerons.
c) mass acting forward of the hinge line.
d) mass acting on the hinge line to keep the surface C of G aft of the hinge.

28. High speed aileron flutter may be reduced on a high aspect ratio wing with:-

a) inboard ailerons which are locked out at the cruise.
b) outboard ailerons which are locked out at the cruise.
c) employment of frise ailerons.
d) the fitting of differential ailerons.

29. Which of the following are forms of aerodynamic balance?:-

a) Horn and Frise
b) Horn and Hinge.
c) Mach Trim and Weight attached to the surface.
d) Weights attached to the surface.

30. In a power 'ON' glide:-

a) lift is equal to weight.
b) thrust is less than drag.
c) the total reaction equals weight.
d) only profile drag is produced.

31. An aileron can be considered to be a flap type control, and when deflected downwards will:-

a) only cause induced drag to be increased.
b) cause profile drag only to be increased.
c) cause both induced and profile drag to be increased together with an increase in the coefficient of lift.
d) increase lift coefficient in that area without drag penalty.

32. A secondary (or further effect) of application of left rudder in level flight would be:-

a) yaw to the right.
b) roll to the right.
c) yaw to the left.
d) roll to the left.

33. The purpose of fitting a Spring Tab to a control surface is:-

a) to reduce a possible tendency of control surface flutter at high speeds.
b) to provide feel (feed back) in a control system.
c) to reduce the effort required in moving the controls at high indicated airspeeds.
d) to provide a constant spring tension in a trim control system.

34. If an aircraft has a tendency to fly right wing low in normal flight, to reduce that tendency:-

a)   a balance tab on the right aileron would need to be moved down.
b)   a trim tab on the right aileron would need to be moved down.
c)   a balance tab on the left aileron would move up.
d)   a trim tab on the left aileron would be required to move down.

35. Which of the following will determine the effectiveness of a control surface of a given shape or size?:-

a)   the distance of the control surface from the aircraft C of G.
b)   TAS and angle of deflection.
c)   the square of the TAS and angle of deflection.
d)   the angle of deflection, the square of the EAS, and the distance of the surface from the aircraft C of G.

36. Control surface overbalance may be the result of:-

a)   movement of the control surface C of P forward of the surface hinge line.
b)   applying excessive force to the control.
c)   movement of the control surface C of P aft of the surface hinge line.
d)   detachment of control surface mass balance weights.

37. Adverse aileron yaw resulting from rolling the aircraft to port (the left) in flight may be reduced by:-

a)   increasing the profile drag produced by the left aileron.
b)   increasing the profile drag produced by the right aileron.
c)   increasing the induced drag produced by the right aileron.
d)   equalising the induced drag produced by both wings.

38. To counteract a nose down attitude in level flight, on an aircraft fitted with a variable incidence tailplane, what action is required?:-

a)   The tailplane trim tab is required to be moved down.
b)   The tailplane leading edge is required to move down.
c)   The tailplane leading edge is required to move up.
d)   The tailplane trim tab is required to be moved up.

39. Failure of a 'Q' Feel Unit in flight will result in:-

a)   increased required effort to move the controls.
b)   loss of Primary Control Systems.
c)   loss of all resistance in moving the controls.
d)   a large reduction in the effort required to move the controls.

40. When an aircraft is in a state of autorotation:-

a)   the inner wing only is fully stalled.
b)   the outer wing only is fully stalled.
c)   the fin only is fully stalled.
d)   both wings are fully stalled.

41. The principle reason for employing wing sweep on an aircraft is to:-

a) delay M_{crit}
b) advance M_{crit}
c) improve high and low speed handling characteristics.
d) alleviate wing tip stall at high speeds.

PROPELLERS

42. The Thrust Face of a propeller blade:-

a) is the flat face.
b) is the cambered face.
c) is the rear face.
d) is the front face only when positive pitch is applied.

43. The centrifugal Turning or Twisting Moment on a propeller will tend to:-

a) cause the blade to move to coarse pitch when rotating.
b) cause the blade to move to fine pitch when rotating.
c) cause the blade to pitch lock in neutral when rotating.
d) cause the blade to feather when oil supply pressure fails.

44. In a single acting constant speed propeller, the actuator spring:-

a) opposes the CSU weights.
b) moves the propeller through coarse to feather.
c) moves the propeller through a coarse to fine pitch.
d) moves the propeller out of the feathered position, when selected.

45. During normal operation, the forces to which a propeller is subjected are:-

a) thrust, torsion and compression.
b) thrust, centrifugal and compression.
c) thrust, centrifugal and shear.
d) thrust, centrifugal and torsion.

46. The plane of rotation of a propeller is:-

a) the angle at which the blades strike the air.
b) the plane in which the thrust forces are said to act.
c) the plane in which the propeller rotates.
d) the axis through which the propeller rotates.

47. Why is a propeller blade manufactured with a state of twist from root to tip?:-

a) to maintain a constant angle of attack from root to tip during normal operation.
b) to ensure that the maximum thrust generated is always greatest at the blade root.
c) to reduce the torsional load at the blade root.
d) to assist in moving the blades into feather if the engine fails.

48. The purpose of the CSU oil booster pump, of a variable pitch propeller, is to:-

    a)   lubricate the constant speed unit.
    b)   increase the engine oil pressure for propeller operation.
    c)   increase engine oil pressure for feathering operations.
    d)   unfeather the propeller.

49. On an aircraft fitted with a variable pitch propeller, if engine rev/min are to remain constant when engine power is increased, it requires:-

    a)   a decrease in blade angle.
    b)   an increase in blade angle.
    c)   a decrease in angle of attack.
    d)   a constant angle of attack to be maintained.

50. A propeller mounted forward of the engine is termed:-

    a)   a pusher propeller.
    b)   a paddle propeller.
    c)   a tractor propeller.
    d)   a hydropneumatic propeller.

ANSWERS

1. - d	26. - b
2. - b	27. - c
3. - c	28. - b
4. - e	29. - b
5. - a	30. - b
6. - c	31. - c
7. - b	32. - d
8. - d	33. - c
9. - d	34. - d
10. - a	35. - d
11. - b	36. - a
12. - d	37. - a
13. - d	38. - b
14. - a	39. - d
15. - b	40. - a
16. - c	41. - a
17. - c	42. - b
18. - a	43. - b
19. - b	44. - b
20. - c	45. - d
21. - b	46. - c
22. - c	47. - a
23. - d	48. - b
24. - a	49. - b
25. - a	50. - c

1. At the propelling nozzle of a gas turbine engine:-

   a) gas velocity increases, pressure increases and temperature reduces.
   b) gas pressure and temperature increase and velocity reduces.
   c) gas velocity increases, pressure reduces and temperature increases.
   d) gas velocity, pressure and temperature are controlled to give optimum conditions.

2. The thrust reverser in a High By-pass engine reverses the flow:-

   a) of hot and cold air by reversing the pitch of the LP compressor blades.
   b) of the hot gas by means of blocking the normal outlet, causing reverse flow through the engine.
   c) by blocking the normal outlet of LP compressor air in the by-pass.
   d) by using HP air in the by-pass duct and deflecting it through cascade vanes.

3. The oil cooler of a piston engine lubrication system is fitted:-

   a) at the front of the engine and between the scavange pump and tank.
   b) at the front of the engine and between the pressure pump and tank.
   c) at the back of the engine and between the scavange pump and tank.
   d) at the back of the engine and between the pressure pump and tank.

4. AVGAS 100LL has a lower lead content than 100L and is therefore identified:-

   a) by low lead painted on the cap of the fuel tank.
   b) by smell and its light straw colour.
   c) by a black square with 100LL painted in red on the aircraft.
   d) with a blue coloured dye in the fuel.

5. If, when in a climb, the waste gate actuator outlet port becomes blocked in a turbocharged piston engine, what will happen to the waste gate?:-

   a) It will fully close and the engine may be overboosted.
   b) It will fully open and engine power will rapidly reduce.
   c) It will fully close and will achieve a much lower critical altitude.
   d) It will fully close and engine power will reduce.

6. In a multi combuster gas turbine engine, how many igniters are fitted?:-

   a) one igniter per combustion chamber.
   b) two igniters per combustion chamber.
   c) two igniters in two combustion chambers.
   d) one igniter per combustion chamber and two stand-by igniters for emergency ignition.

7. On a single spool axial flow compressor, where are the dump valves located?:-

   a)   at the LP end of the compressor.
   b)   at the HP end of the compressor.
   c)   at an intermediate point between the LP and HP ends of the compressor.
   d)   at the inlet to the compressor.

8. In a twin spool high by-pass engine at cruise rpm, what are the relative speeds of the Low and High compressor spools?:-

   a)   The LP and HP compressors rotate at the same rpm.
   b)   The LP compressor rotates at higher rpm than the HP compressor.
   c)   The HP compressor rotates at a higher rpm than the low pressure compressor.
   d)   the HP compressor rotates at the same rpm as the intermediate compressor.

9. The capsule of an Automatic Boost Control Unit is sensitive to:-

   a)   ambient.
   b)   manifold pressure.
   c)   throttle inputs and ambient.
   d)   pitot static pressure.

10. In which part of a Gas Turbine Engine is the temperature greatest?:-

   a)   Inlet Guide Vanes.
   b)   Nozzle Guide Vanes.
   c)   Propelling Nozzle.
   d)   Exhaust.

11. Relight in a gas turbine engine, after a flame out, is most likely to be successful:-

   a)   at high speed.
   b)   at a height below 25000 ft.
   c)   at a height above 25000 ft.
   d)   at any altitude at low speed.

12. An APU is:-

   a)   ram air driven.
   b)   a small gas turbine engine.
   c)   electrically driven.
   d)   hydraulically driven.

13. Static Boost in a supercharged engine is:-

   a)   'O' boost when the aircraft is stationary.
   b)   'O' boost when the aircraft is at sea level, with the engine switched off.
   c)   never 'O' boost
   d)   'O' boost when the aircraft is stationary, at sea level with the engine switched off in ISA conditions.

14. Pitot Static inputs for EFIS instrumentation are transmitted to the instruments via:-

   a)   the FMS.
   b)   the Manometric Computer.
   c)   the Air Data Computer
   d)   the Auto Flight Computer.

15. An EFIS Installation consists of:-

   a)   four screens and two symbol generators.
   b)   two screens and one symbol generator.
   c)   two screens, one control panel and two symbol generators.
   d)   four screens and three symbol generators.

16. In which of the following logic gates are contained the six most common gates?:-

   a)   NAND, NOR, EXOR.
   b)   AND, NOR, NAND.
   c)   NAND, INHIBITED AND, and OR.
   d)   OR, NAND and NOT.

17. During Autoland Alert condition below Alert Height:-

   a)   display is LAND 1 and the landing should be aborted.
   b)   display is Fail Operational and this can be ignored.
   c)   display is Alert and the landing should be carried out manually with runway visual.
   d)   autoland may continue using stand-by instruments.

18. The Autoland Status is displayed:-

   a)   on the EHSI at all times.
   b)   on the EADI at all times.
   c)   on the EADI when autoland is selected.
   d)   on the EHSI when autoland is selected.

19. Which of the following are considered advantages of using tubeless tyre assemblies on aircraft compared to a tubed tyre?:-

   a)   They are cooler in operation when subjected to high speeds and high loads.
   b)   They operate at higher temperatures and so provide better grip.
   c)   They are not capable of blow-outs during operation.
   d)   They permit easier wheel change.

20. Prior to landing, what considerations should be given to the aircraft tyres?:-

   a)   Tyre pressures, aircraft mass, and runway surface conditions.
   b)   Aircraft mass, landing speed, and tyre pressures.
   c)   Aircraft mass, tyre pressures and type of tyre tread.
   d)   Aircraft mass, runway conditions and landing speed.

21. An aircraft tyre is strongest:-

    a)   when under dynamic load, below maximum rated speed.
    b)   when under static load.
    c)   when under static load, but at normal operating temperature.
    d)   when under dynamic load throughout its operating temperature range.

22. In a hydraulic system fitted with a constant volume pump, when maximum system pressure is reached:-

    a)   the pump off loads completely.
    b)   the pump maintains a small leak rate through the pump, whilst in the off load position.
    c)   the pump is disengaged by a pressure operated clutch.
    d)   an idling circuit is created via the reservoir.

23. The purpose of an accumulator in a hydraulic system is to:-

    a)   compensate for thermal expansion.
    b)   prevent cavitation at the main pump.
    c)   damp out surges in the system.
    d)   prevent cavitation at the reservoir.

24. What is the purpose of a flop tube, as fitted to a hydraulic reservoir?:-

    a)   To prevent total loss of fluid in the event of leakage in the main supply.
    b)   To compensate for changes in aircraft attitude.
    c)   To pressurise the hydraulic reservoir.
    d)   To compensate for thermal expansion.

25. What type of hydraulic seal will seal in one direction only?:-

    a)   Square Section.
    b)   Chevron.
    c)   'O' Section.
    d)   Diamond Section

26. What is the purpose of a pressure switch in a hydraulic supply system?:-

    a)   To operate the pressure gauge.
    b)   To switch off the pump when maximum pressure is reached.
    c)   To prevent excess pressure build-up in the system.
    d)   To operate a warning light in the event of system pressure failure.

27. Red mineral based hydraulic fluid (DTD 585) requires:-

    a)   natural rubber seals.
    b)   fibre seals.
    c)   mineral seals.
    d)   synthetic rubber seals.

28. What is the purpose of the Beta Range of a propeller?:-

   a)   For take-off at high temperatures.
   b)   To move the propeller blades to feather in an emergency.
   c)   For ground manoeuvring.
   d)   To bring the propeller out of feather.

29. Why are propeller blades twisted?:-

   a)   To maintain a constant angle of attack along the length of the blade during operation.
   b)   To maintain aerodynamic stability at low rpm.
   c)   To assist the blade to absorb stress during operation.
   d)   To prevent the propeller overspeeding.

30. An aerodynamic force on a propeller blade, which tends to turn the blade to coarse pitch during operation, is termed:-

   a)   CTM.
   b)   Beta.
   c)   Slip.
   d)   ATM.

31. A mechanically driven pump, contained within a propeller constant speed unit, is fitted to:-

   a)   feather the propeller, and is called the Feathering Pump.
   b)   boost the feathering pump oil pressure, and is called the Booster Pump.
   c)   Increase engine oil pressure for propeller operation and is called the Booster Pump.
   d)   Feather the propeller and is called the Emergency Pump.

32. In cruise flight conditions, a propellers ATM is:-

   a)   equal to its CTM. (Centrifugal Twisting Moment)
   b)   greater than its CTM.
   c)   equal to its DTM (Dynamic Turning Moment)
   d)   less than its CTM.

33. When the flyweights of the propeller CSU, during operation, move outwards overcoming the spring force:-

   a)   the propeller is ON SPEED.
   b)   the propeller is UNDERSPEEDING.
   c)   the propeller is OVERSPEEDING.
   d)   the propeller is PITCH-LOCKED.

34. When there is no movement of oil to or from the actuator of a variable pitch, constant speed propeller during operation, the propeller is:-

   a)   pitch locked.
   b)   on speed.
   c)   underspeeding.
   d)   overspeeding.

35. Where are the nozzle guide vanes located within a gas turbine engine?:-

a) In the primary zone of the combustion chamber.
b) Downstream of the combustion chamber.
c) Upstream of the swirl vanes.
d) At the inlet to the compressor.

36. Gas turbine engine main bearings are lubricated by a continuous recirculating system using:-

a) mineral based oil.
b) natural based oil.
c) synthetic oil.
d) vegetable based oil.

37. Which of the following will cause an APU to automatically shut down?:-

a) High EGT and low oil pressure.
b) Excessive EGT and open squat switches on take off.
c) Low rpm and high EGT.
d) Closed squat switches and high rpm.

38. Gas turbine inter stage bleed valves:-

a) are open when the nozzle guide vanes are open.
b) are closed when the variable inlet guide vanes are closed.
c) are open when the variable inlet guide vanes are closed.
d) are open when the nozzle guide vanes are closed.

39. A gas turbine engine when started at altitude, compared to sea level, will achieve:-

a) a lower thrust at a higher idle rpm.
b) a higher rpm with greater thrust.
c) a lower thrust with the same rpm.
d) the same idle rpm and thrust.

40. Compared to a single spool turbojet, a high by pass gas turbine engine designed to handle the same mass flow:-

a) will have a greater power to weight ratio.
b) will produce greater thrust.
c) will be shorter with a lower diameter.
d) will be larger and heavier.

41. The output of a turboprop engine is indicated as:-

a) torque.
b) torque and thrust.
c) thrust and rpm.
d) rpm and shp.

42. Gas turbine igniters, when fitted to a multi combuster engine, are supplied with electrical current from:-

   a) at least two magneto's
   b) the batteries direct.
   c) high power ignition units.
   d) the vital bus bar.

43. To reduce instability the blades of the LP compressor of a high by-pass engine are:-

   a) of narrow chord construction and taper from root to tip.
   b) constructed with a parallel chord from root to tip.
   c) of a wide chord construction and taper from root to tip.
   d) manufactured with a wide chord and are parallel from root to tip.

44. Gas turbine engine compressor bleed air, when used to cool nozzle guide vanes is bled from:-

   a) the LP end of the compressor.
   b) a ram air duct in the engine intake.
   c) a by pass duct.
   d) the HP compressor.

45. What is the purpose of the 'Flare' in a combustion chamber of a gas turbine engine?:-

   a) To generate a vortex to atomise the fuel.
   b) To create circulating air in the primary zone.
   c) To provide dilution air to assist in cooling the flame.
   d) To accelerate the airflow in the primary zone.

46. Within the combustion chamber of a gas turbine engine where is the flame located during flight?:-

   a) in the tertiary zone.
   b) at the snout.
   c) in the primary zone.
   d) in the flare.

47. What is the primary function of 'Bogie' or 'Multi Wheel' undercarriage units?:-

   a) To distribute the aircraft mass over a greater area.
   b) To provide safety should a tyre blow out occur.
   c) To allow the undercarriage to be retracted into the wing.
   d) To reduce scuffing of tyres when taxying.

48. In the event the APU shuts down whilst refuelling is being carried out on an aircraft:-

a) it may be restarted immediately and fuelling continued.
b) fuel caps must be replaced and vents closed before the APU is restarted.
c) fuel caps must be replaced before the APU is restarted.
d) The APU cannot be restarted for one hour.

49. To avoid wheel tyre scuffing when taxying, the aircraft speed should be kept to:-

a) a minimum of 22 kts.
b) the maximum rated speed for the tyres.
c) a maximum of 22 kts.
d) the minimum rated speed for the tyres.

50. In a piston engine ignition system the current to the spark plug is supplied:-

a) from the primary coil via the contact points.
b) from the secondary coil via the distributor.
c) from the secondary coil via the ignition switch.
d) direct from the secondary coil.

51. In a piston engine ignition system, failure of a magneto with a lead disconnected from the switch of the other magneto will result in:-

a) the engine continuing to run normally.
b) overheating of the engine.
c) total failure of the engine.
d) a reduction in engine power.

52. When a piston engine reaches normal operating temperature, the presence of blue smoke from its exhaust indicates:-

a) the cylinders are at an excessive temperature.
b) the oil cooler by-pass valve is closed.
c) the oil cooler by-pass valve is open.
d) hydraulicing could be a problem when the engine is next started.

53. Which of the following statements is correct of supercharged piston engines?:-

a) An increase of rpm requires the ignition to be retarded.
b) Rated boost is the maximum obtainable boost.
c) Rated rpm is selected on the power lever.
d) Static boost is always shown as zero boost.

54. Above rated altitude a supercharged engine will:-

a) maintain rated boost in the induction manifold.
b) behave like a normally aspirated engine as altitude is increased.
c) maintain a full throttle height in the induction manifold.
d) experience an increase in exhaust back pressure.

55. Electrical batteries when connected in parallel provide .... amp/hr capacity and .... voltage:-

a) increased - the same.
b) the same - increased.
c) reduced - increased.
d) increased - reduced.

56. During normal cruise flight conditions a Ni-cad battery's ammeter shows a high rate of charge. What does this indicate?:-

a) It can be ignored as it is quite normal.
b) That a high demand is being made on the system.
c) That the generator should be disconnected from the bus bar.
d) That a possible thermal runaway exists.

57. A generator can be said to be 'on line' :-

a) When idle rpm is achieved at engine starting.
b) When the generator reaches its operational rpm.
c) When the generator is connected to the bus bar.
d) When operational excitation is achieved.

58. The letters ECTA marked on the wall of a tyre indicate:-

a) It is a tyre that is manufactured in the EU.
b) It is a high pressure tyre.
c) It is an electrically conducting tyre.
d) It is a steel reinforced tyre.

59. The letters PNP when related to a transistor denote:-

a) Positive - Negative - Positive
b) Positive - Neutral - Positive.
c) Positive - Negative - Positive or Positive - Neutral - Positive.
d) Positive - Negated - Positive.

60. How many diodes are required in a three phase full wave bridge rectifier?:-

a) 3.
b) 1.
c) 4.
d) 6.

61. When the brightness level is selected on the control panel of an EFIS display it is then:-

a) automatically controlled by light sensors which vary the light level on the flight deck.
b) automatically controlled by light sensors which adjust the brightness on the CRT's.
c) further adjusted manually when required.
d) further adjusted manually by adjustment of the flight deck lighting.

62. A rod type turnbuckle, as fitted to a flying control system, is locked:-

a) when not more than three threads are showing.
b) when the inspection holes are obstructed.
c) with locking wire.
d) with stiff nuts.

63. On larger aircraft flying control system cable tension is automatically adjusted by:-

a) turnbuckles.
b) auto-turnbuckles.
c) tensionmeters.
d) tension regulators.

64. Insufficient extension of an oil compression shockstrut, when fitted to an undercarriage with aircraft weight applied, is most probably due to:-

a) low air pressure.
b) low oil level or low air pressure.
c) low oil pressure.
d) low oil pressure and low air pressure.

65. Aircraft flying control cables are manufactured from:-

a) light alloy.
b) stainless steel.
c) steel.
d) copper alloy.

1. - d	33. - c
2. - c	34. - b
3. - a	35. - b
4. - d	36. - c
5. - a	37. - b
6. - c	38. - c
7. - b	39. - a
8. - c	40. - a
9. - b	41. - a
10. - b	42. - c
11. - b	43. - c
12. - b	44. - d
13. - d	45. - b
14. - c	46. - c
15. - d	47. - a
16. - a	48. - b
17. - c	49. - c
18. - c	50. - b
19. - a	51. - d
20. - d	52. - d
21. - b	53. - a
22. - d	54. - b
23. - c	55. - a
24. - b	56. - d
25. - b	57. - c
26. - d	58. - c
27. - d	59. - a
28. - c	60. - d
29. - a	61. - b
30. - d	62. - c
31. - c	63. - d
32. - d	64. - c
	65. - b